WHAT P

"I'm so thankful for this book by Dave Murphy. The message it gives is so vital today—that you don't have to be defined by defeat. So many pastors, leaders, and believers everywhere have a mindset of defeat that holds them back from what God wants to do in them and through them. My prayer is that as you read this book, you'll find a release to see your life how God sees it—destined for victory!" **Dino Rizzo, author of** *Servolution* **and Executive Director of the Association of Related Churches**

"*Undefeated* is the most practical writing on living by faith that I have ever seen. It is profound because it is a forthright, honest, direct, and balanced look at a subject too often left shrouded in mystery or presented as unattainable for the average believer. I truly appreciate Pastor Dave's transparency, often citing his own struggles to live by faith. I have personally lived these principles for more than forty years and am refreshed by this book. I wish it had been available to me at the onset of my own journey of living by faith." **Walt Healy, Founding Pastor, The Church of Grace and Peace**

"This book is a must-read for anyone who wants to see their life go to a new level. Dave Murphy's *Undefeated* reminds us that in order to experience real breakthrough, it starts within our own heart, soul, and mind. If you are ready to experience everything God has prepared for you, then this book is for you." **Isaac Friedel, Lead Pastor, Shore Christian Church**

"*Undefeated* is a powerful and much-needed anthem of a book that encourages and empowers us to live in victory over our doubts and defeats. Dave's thoughts are provoking and personal—dig in!" **Chris Goeppner, Lead Pastor, Riverbank Church**

"Dave Murphy has written a masterpiece and a comprehensive blueprint to help people of all walks of life experience a victorious lifestyle. *Undefeated* is a must-read. I especially love how simple, clear and practical it is, yet there is depth and plenty of 'Aha!' moments! It's biblically-sound and engaging. Above all, I can assure you that Dave lives out the principles he's sharing in this book." **Zenzo Matoga, Founding Pastor, Impact Church**

"I love being inspired by what I read. But more than inspiration, I covet practical steps to help me apply what I'm learning. Pastor Dave lays out 15 Victory Principles that are simple and helpful to living undefeated, no matter where you are in your spiritual journey." **Dan Stauffer, Relational Network Pastor, Next Level Church**

"I just finished reading the manuscript of Dave's new book, *Undefeated*, and just...wow! As I read, I was personally uplifted and refilled with a hopeful awareness that I was created to win in life—I seriously couldn't put it down. Dave is a seasoned pastor with decades of experience, and his approach in this book is fresh, practical, and encouraging. The stories and testimonies he shares are relevant, life-giving, and hope-filled. I recommend *Undefeated* as a must-read for people from every walk of life. As a lead pastor, I'm going to be buying copies of this book for our congregation. Check it out—you will be launched into a lifestyle of victory." **Jeremie Hamby, Lead Pastor, People's Church**

UNDEFEATED

CONQUERING YOUR DOUBTS AND LIVING IN GOD'S FULLNESS

DAVID MURPHY

Copyright © 2019 by David Murphy

All rights reserved.

No part of this book may be reproduced in any form or by any electronic or mechanical means, including information storage and retrieval systems, without written permission from the author, except for the use of brief quotations in a book review.

To Raquel, my one true love and partner in the undefeated life for more than twenty years.

ACKNOWLEDGMENTS

I am greatly indebted to those who have sown seeds of faith in me. Thank you for believing in me and challenging me to live the undefeated life. Special thanks to Dewey, Otto, Ken, Dan, Deryck, Layne, Matt and Tim, as well as Mom and Dad Murphy and Mom and Dad Pérez.

CONTENTS

Introduction	xi
1. Change Your Thinking	1
2. A Faith Bias	15
3. Upgrade Your Morning	27
4. Speak Life	39
5. Discover Praise	51
6. God First	65
7. It Never Gets Old	77
8. The New You	89
9. Watch What You Eat	101
10. Win the War	113
11. Your Secret Weapon	127
12. Freedom in Forgiveness	139
13. We > Me	151
14. Living to Give	163
15. Living to Serve	175
Epilogue	187
Notes	189
About the Author	191
Coming Soon	193

INTRODUCTION

GOD WANTS YOU to live in victory. Jesus didn't die so you would live a mediocre, barely-getting-by life. God has great things for your future—you just need to get ready! It's easy to miss what God has for our lives because we get distracted or lulled to sleep by the cares of life. I read about a burglar in Scotland who fell asleep in the house he had broken into, after eating half a pie and a bag of Doritos. Police tweeted that "he woke up in handcuffs" and added the hashtag "#fingerlickinggood."[1]

Fifteen Victory Principles

I know you want to get ready and stay ready for all that God has for your life. This book was written for you to live the undefeated life. It's possible to live a life of continual victory, despite the difficulties or trials you face. God doesn't want you to take one step forward and two steps back. He wants you to learn principles that will move you forward in spite of your struggles. Maybe you've been betrayed, or treated unfairly, or you're still waiting on your physical or financial breakthrough. In all these things, you can still be more than a conqueror. My prayer for you is that you learn to apply the fifteen victory principles in this book, and that you begin to live the undefeated life. Each chapter details one victory principle, and there is a discussion guide at the end of every chapter to help you process what you are learning with a friend or a small group.

Have you suffered a setback? There is still victory ahead for you. Have you received a bad report? There is victory ahead for you. Have you just about given up? There is still victory ahead for you. Each of these fifteen victory principles has been time-tested and proven true in my own life and in the lives of the people I pastor. None of these principles is magical—they won't make your problems disappear in a day. They require hard work and faith and determination. But if you set your mind to apply each principle to your own life, I promise you that victory will come. It may take time, but it will come.

My Journey Towards Victory

I must confess that I have not always lived the undefeated life. There have been stretches of failure and defeat and depression in my life, and the victory principles I am going to share with you have been hard-won and battle-tested. I remember a time when I was driving my car alone at night and talking to God. Well, complaining, actually.

"I don't know why I bother, Lord. I try to do your will and I just fall further behind financially. And now I've got these people betraying me. And besides that, work is killing me." In my funk, I flipped around the radio stations and a preacher came on. I was just about to change the station, because I was looking for classic rock, not church, but the preacher said something that arrested me.

"Joseph didn't do anything wrong, but he ended up in prison. He had every reason to complain, but he didn't. He kept waking up every morning and thanking God for a new day. He kept putting God first and doing the right thing. It's possible that the difficulty you are facing right now is not the result of your sin. It's possible you are doing the right thing and the enemy just wants to discourage you. Keep fighting and keep believing God for victory, and He will bring you out to a place of increased favor and blessing."

"Wow, that was timely," I thought. "I need that Joseph spirit." I asked God to give me the attitude of Joseph and teach me to live in continual victory like Joseph lived. When I got home, I embarked on a quest to learn all that I could about victory, studying the Scripture and reading books and listening to speakers on the topic. It became a decade-long hobby of mine. The book you hold in your hands is the result of those years of study.

Time-Tested Principles

As the lead pastor of a growing church, I have taught hundreds of people these victory principles, and I've seen the amazing effects in their lives. They work! Bianca came to my church defeated and tired. At lunch with my wife and me, Bianca explained how she had just come through a divorce and was tired of struggling in life. She longed for a breakthrough and wasn't sure if God had better for her. We assured her that God had much better for her, in fact, God had an undefeated life for her if she would begin to put Him first and apply His Word consistently. She seemed half-convinced, but agreed to stick around church and join a small group. As God would have it, the teaching series we were starting the very next Sunday dealt with the topic of victory. Bianca never missed a service, and over the weeks, I noticed a change in her countenance. She went from downcast to delighted.

"You were speaking directly to me today!" she told me one morning after church. "I can't express to you the difference this teaching is making in my life." Since that time, Bianca has deepened her relationship with God and seen Him work miracles in her life. She is free from her past and moving forward. And her son, who was far from God for many years, is now attending our church and happily serving the Lord.

Brian is another example of someone who came to our church skeptical and defeated. He wasn't into God, as he'd had some negative church experiences in the past. But he couldn't deny the positive changes he saw in his wife after she rededicated her life to Christ at our church. She stopped cursing and fussing, and began to walk in a peace that he wanted for himself. Over coffee, he told me that his biggest problem was his own head.

"I am my own worst enemy," he confided. "I can't stop thinking negative thoughts, no matter how hard I try." I shared with him what the Bible says about his new identity in Christ and how old things have passed away and all things become new in Christ. "That sounds great," he said, "but how do I keep those good thoughts in my head?" he asked.

"Over time you will learn to replace your thoughts with God's thoughts. Keep showing up and taking notes and asking questions," I said. "You'll get there." One year later, Brian reached a place of consistent victory in his life. He learned to think God's thoughts and close the door to defeatist thinking. At his water baptism, he said, "I can't imagine my life without Jesus now. I love serving Him, and am so blessed, just feeling complete in Him."

Victory is Your Birthright

The Bible says categorically that God "gives us the victory through our Lord Jesus Christ" (1 Cor. 15:57). Victory is the birthright of all those who are in Christ. That means it's yours, whether you deserve it or not. It's yours by way of birth. Not your natural birth, but your new birth in Christ. Victory is God's design for His church. There is no enemy, no obstacle, no struggle that should conquer us. Will we have difficulties and challenges? Of course we will. But in all these things we overwhelmingly conquer through Him who loves us.

May this book be your companion in your journey towards the undefeated life. May you live the life that God intended for you when He sent His Son to die for you and give you the abundant, overcoming, undefeated life. May your victory shine so brightly that it saturates all those around you.

"For the Lord your God is he who goes with you to fight for you against your enemies, to give you the victory" (Deut. 20:4).

1
CHANGE YOUR THINKING

"You cannot have a positive life and a negative mind."—Joyce Meyer

THE AFTERNOON SUN shone pleasantly on my face, but I didn't notice. I was in the on-deck circle going through my warm-up routine, next in line to hit for my Little League baseball team. I swung the weighted bat and blocked out the rest of the world. "This year will be different," I told myself. The previous year had been frustrating. My coach believed in me, but I stopped believing in myself. When you strike out a lot, it gets into your head. On the way home from a particularly dismal game, my dad offered me this advice:

"You've got to *believe*, Dave. When you get up to the plate, you've already defeated yourself. If you think you're going to strike out, you will. Before you step up to that plate, see the ball hitting the bat. Believe you're going to hit the ball, and you'll hit it for sure." The previous season ended before I could implement my dad's advice, but this new season was a fresh start. Now that I stood in the on-deck circle preparing to approach the plate on that sunny afternoon, I closed my eyes and saw the ball hitting the bat.

"This year will be different. I'm going to hit that ball!" I approached the plate, dug in my cleats, tapped the plate once with my bat, and waited for the first pitch. It was a high fastball and I swung. I instantly felt the crack of a perfect connection between bat and ball. The ball sailed over the shortstop's head as I ran towards first base with that delightful mix of feelings: "Did I just do that?" and "Darn right I just did that!" My hit allowed the winning run to score for our team, and I became the hero for a night. My dad let me eat chocolate chip mint ice cream before dinner, and announced to the whole family, "Now *that's* the way you do it!"

Sometimes you learn life lessons on the baseball diamond. I learned that if you change your thinking, everything else changes.

Change Your Thinking, Change Your Life

Your thinking has a dramatic effect on your life. Your level of victory as a follower of Jesus often depends on your mindset. To live undefeated, learn to think undefeated. It's not an exaggeration to say that if you change your thinking, your whole life will change.

"But I can't change my thinking," you might say. Yes, you can. You are not a powerless victim. God has given you the tools and the ability to alter your thought patterns. It won't happen overnight, but you can experience true freedom through undefeated thinking.

I have a friend who spent years addicted to alcohol. Through a twelve-step program and the Word of God, he is now free. "It's a daily struggle, Pastor Dave," he recently told me. "But I'm free. My biggest enemy, by far, is this right here," he said, pointing to his head. "I still have to retrain my thinking every morning, reminding myself of certain truths and rejecting old, familiar lies. That's the only thing I've found that works to keep me in victory."

That sounds like undefeated thinking to me. Retrain your thinking every morning!

Start at the Right Starting Line

I'm a runner, and I've run many 5k and 10k races. One time, I almost started a race from the wrong spot. I was with a group of runners who had warmed up and were waiting for the start, when one of them said, "Hey, is that the starting line down there?" We all freaked out and ran down to where he was pointing. We arrived just in time for the official start of the race!

When we identify a problem area in our lives that we want to fix, we can make the mistake of trying to start from the wrong starting line. Ironically, the starting point for changing your thinking is not your own mind. The starting point is located outside your head, rooted in the eternal, changeless promises of God. Don't start your undefeated journey by looking inward; look upward and outward to Jesus and all that he has done for you. When you look inward, you despair because you're a mess. When you look upward, you rejoice because Jesus has already redeemed your mess.

When you read the Apostle Paul's beautiful words, "But thanks be to God, who gives us the victory through our Lord Jesus Christ" (1 Cor. 15:57), you need to notice the 'but.' Yes, a preacher just told you to notice the 'but!' Paul is saying that our victory in Christ is in the context of something darker. In the previous verses, Paul discusses the death and pain we all face. He readily admits that death and difficulty are part of our existence, this side of heaven. That's when he introduces the 'but.' Paul says, "Yes, you will have darkness and difficulty and even death, *but* don't despair, in all these things, you are more than a conqueror in Christ!"

Our focus should never be on the sin and death that surround us. Our focus should be on the victory given to us. *That is the starting line!* Shift your thinking. Make the shift from defeated to victorious, from failing to winning, from down to up, in Jesus' name. Every morning, start your day by reminding yourself of all that Jesus has done for you: He has saved you, forgiven you, given you a new life here on earth and heaven for all eternity, filled you with his Holy Spirit, given you His

Word with answers to all of life's questions, provided all of your needs according to His riches in glory, imbued you with a calling and a purpose, and surrounded you with good people who believe like you do.

Your Victory is Already Given

In the Christian life, you start from a place of victory—you are not trying to attain a place of victory. The victory was given to you on the cross. It is finished—it's yours. Don't try to earn it. Just receive it and rejoice in it. Jesus already did all the work. Your job is to clothe yourself in His victory and thank Him for it.

I was once given a free two-day pass to an indoor water park resort in Pennsylvania. My wife and I had seen the pictures online, but when our four kids walked into the wilderness lodge reception area with the huge stone fireplace, they began to get excited. When they saw the wolf den bedroom suite, they said, "Wow, Dad!" But when they saw the ridiculously massive indoor water park, they totally lost it. It took me half an hour to calm them down enough to change into their bathing suits! Later that evening, I stopped by the front desk. I wanted to see how much one night in our room cost. To my surprise, the price was $400 per night.

"Four hundred dollars?" I said. "Good Lord, no wonder we never come here!"

But, of course, I wasn't paying for our stay. We had been given the two nights for free. I didn't earn them. I just received them and enjoyed the benefit of them. The same thing is true of your victory in Christ. You didn't earn it. You simply receive it and enjoy the benefits of it.

Jesus conquered every enemy so you can walk in victory. The sin and guilt that separated you from God? Conquered. Your fear of the future? Conquered. Your mental torment? Conquered. Your greatest enemy, death? Conquered. You are walking in the victory parade of Someone else who already conquered all your enemies. That's what the Apostle Paul means when he says that God "always leads us in triumphal procession" (2 Cor. 2:14). Jesus won the victory for you—enjoy the parade!

Don't be like those Christians who are not enjoying the parade. Jesus won the victory for them, but they are not experiencing it. They don't feel it, they don't taste it. It all seems like a faraway dream. If that describes you at all, then this book is for you. Your birthright as a follower of Jesus is not subpar living, halfway victories and occasional wins. God wants you to experience victory in every and any situation of your life. Whatever the challenge, whatever the struggle, you can experience the victory that Jesus won for you on the cross. You can live the undefeated life.

The Voice of Negativity

To live undefeated, you must conquer the voice of negativity. In my own life, that negative voice began to speak to me at a young age.

"That will never work."

"You've tried and failed before."

"Everyone else is better than you."

"Nobody likes you."

The voice would get louder anytime I was trying something new or stepping outside of my comfort zone.

"You are not good at that."

"Maybe you should sit down and stick to what you are good at."

And when something went wrong in my life? Yeah, the voice of negativity had something to say about that, too.

"See? I knew it! It's always the same thing. You might as well give up."

This voice spoke to me unchecked until I became a Christian at age nineteen. All of a sudden, my thinking began to change. The more I read the words of Jesus, the more the voice of negativity seemed wrong. Jesus wasn't negative. None of the New Testament writers were negative. They constantly spoke of faith and hope and life and redemption and a better future. I saw that *victory* was the theme of the whole New Testament.

> "I came that they may have life and have it abundantly" (John 10:10).
> "But thanks be to God, who in Christ always leads us in triumphal procession" (2 Cor 2:14).
> "In all these things we are more than conquerors through him who loved us" (Rom 8:37).
> "But thanks be to God, who gives us the victory through our Lord Jesus Christ" 1 Cor 15:57).

If the theme of the New Testament is victory in Christ, what was I going to do with my negativity? I saw that victory and negativity don't get along very well. In fact, they can't stand to be in the same room together. As I filled my mind with the positive, faith-filled words of Scripture, my old friend negativity stopped coming around. He knew that he wasn't welcome anymore.

"From now on," I decided, "I'm going to think God's thoughts. I hereby reject the voice of negativity and will not entertain those old thoughts anymore."

I made a decision, and you can, too. I changed my mindset from failure to victory. I said to myself, "If Jesus has already given me the victory, I will start applying it and walking in it." I made the decision to shut down the negative and fire up the positive.

Five Keys to Change Your Thinking

Of course, it wasn't easy. Changing my thinking didn't happen overnight. It was a process that I had to work at diligently over time. But I succeeded in changing my thinking, and you can, too. Here are five keys that will help you in the process of changing your thinking from defeated to undefeated.

. . .

ONE: Focus on the Word. The Bible is your handbook for victory. Saturate yourself in the Scripture. The Bible has a life-giving quality to it that no other book has. The key to changing your mindset from negative to undefeated is getting the Word in you and believing it. I recommend that you make the Bible your morning's top priority. There are many other things you could do with your time, but none of them will have as great an impact on your thinking as getting the Word in you first thing in the morning. Start your day with the promises of God, and your mindset will shift from defeated to victorious, from doubting to believing.

Over the years, I have met many people who have experienced the life-giving power of the Word. John was one of the most memorable. He was a white-haired Irishman from Brooklyn who led our Monday night men's Bible study. He opened the meeting the same way every week. "Remember fellas, John 15:7 says, 'If you abide in me, and my words abide in you, ask whatever you wish, and it will be done for you.'" You might think it would get annoying to hear the same verse quoted every week. But it didn't, because it came from John. He was so clearly living what he preached that it inspired us. We looked forward to the energy John brought into the room. Something about his passion made us want what he had. I never caught John on a bad day. He was always confessing the Word and believing God for something great.

"How do people like John stay positive all the time?" I wondered. We met at a diner once for breakfast, and I asked John myself.

"I stay in the Word," he answered. "It's that simple. I wake up with the Bible and go to sleep with the Bible in my heart and mind and in my mouth. You see, apart from God, I am not a positive guy. Before I met Jesus, I was a rough character, running the streets, raising hell. I was foul-mouthed and extremely negative. That's just the way I grew up. When you're surrounded by so much junk in your life, it's easy to be negative."

"So what changed you?" I asked.

"I didn't become a follower of Jesus until I was forty-two," John replied. "At that point, I realized that I had wasted much of my life on negativity, and my time was slipping away. So I determined to use every single day God gives me to praise Him and bring honor to His name."

"Was it hard to change your thinking?" I asked.

"It sure was!" John said with a laugh. "My negativity was rooted deep within me. I asked my wife to keep me accountable and call me out on every negative word that came out of my mouth. I began to memorize Scripture verses so I could say them out loud every time I had a negative thought. I memorized sixty verses that way!"

"So, saturating your mind with Scripture broke the hold of negativity over your mind?" I asked.

"That's the secret," he replied. "And believe me, nothing else works. I've tried everything else. Only Scripture has the power to set you free and keep you free."

If God can transform the thinking of a rough Brooklynite and make him the most positive person I know, what can he do in your life?

TWO: Chase down your negative thoughts. Your negative thoughts try to hide unnoticed in the corners of your mind. They pretend to be your friends, and you will almost believe them because they've been with you for so long. But they are not your friends. They need to be exposed for what they are: toxic lies. Chase down your negative thoughts and kick them out of your head.

If you ever have thoughts like, "God is sick of me and doesn't love people like me," or "I will never get better," or "Everybody hates me," or "I'm being punished for a past life," then you need to do some thought chasing. Don't let those lies live in your head! You can't make progress in the undefeated life if you allow the enemy camp rent-free in your head.

Kicking the enemy's lies out of your head is a two-step process:

1. Identify the lie.
2. Replace it with truth.

First, you need to identify the lie. Grab the thought, hold it up to the light, and assess whether it's true or not. As you integrate more Scripture into your thinking, it will become easier to do this accurately. Once you identify the lie, insist on replacing it with God's truth. Remember the phrase, "It is written."

Jesus shows us exactly how to do this in Luke 4. He is just about to begin His public ministry. The devil dispenses with the formalities and launches an all-out frontal attack on Him. He tempts Jesus to break His forty-day fast and feed Himself. Jesus was waiting on the Father's instructions, not the devil's, so He tells the enemy, "It is written, 'Man shall not live by bread alone'" (v. 4). Jesus identifies the lie and replaces it with the truth. The devil's lie was that Jesus could function outside of the Father's instructions and make His own decisions. It was a tempting lie, but Jesus didn't allow it to live in His head for one second. "Get out of here, devil. I will stick to what's written."

Then the devil takes Jesus to a high mountain and shows Him all the kingdoms of the world. He offers to give Jesus all this glory, if the Son of God would fall down and worship him. Jesus answers, "It is written, 'You shall worship the Lord your God, and him only shall you serve'" (v. 8). The lie was that Jesus could have a shortcut to glory. Forget about all the sacrifice and suffering, jump right to the good part. It was certainly a tempting proposition, but once again, Jesus identifies the lie and replaces it with the truth. "I don't think so, devil. I will do it God's way."

Finally, the devil takes Jesus to the pinnacle of the temple and quotes Scripture to him. He goads Jesus to throw himself down, since the Bible promises that God's angels will protect you from all harm. Jesus answers that it is also written, "You shall not put the Lord your God to the test" (v. 12). The lie was that Jesus could attract attention to His ministry using fleshly and self-focused methods. That certainly sounds better than getting beaten and dying on a cross, doesn't it? But once again, Jesus identifies the lie and replaces it with the truth. "Give it up, devil. I reject your lies and stand in the truth."

What is the one phrase you hear from Jesus' lips in all three temptations? "It is written." If the Son of God quoted Scripture in His battle with the enemy, how much more should we? Just like Jesus, you can learn to identify the enemy's lies as soon as they come into your mind and replace them with the truth of God's Word. The devil laughs at your opinions but flees at the sound of Scripture.

THREE: Stop opening doors. You have the ability to open mental doors to negative thinking or to slam them shut. Don't be surprised if the enemy is messing with your head if you are opening the door to toxic thought patterns. Be wise and selective with what you watch and listen to. All of our thinking is influenced by books we read, videos we watch, songs we listen to, and people we talk to. It's natural and inevitable to have our thinking influenced by the voices we pay attention to. Ask yourself, "What voices do I give attention to in my life? Are they healthy or toxic?"

One time, a teenage girl came to me and said, "Pastor Dave, I can't sleep at night. I'm having horrible nightmares." As we spoke, the Holy Spirit prompted me to ask her if she was watching horror movies. "Um, yeah," she replied. "I watched a really scary movie before going to bed last night. Do you think that has anything to do with it?"

Um, yeah! I told her to stop opening the doors of her mind to that negative influence, and one week later, she came back and told me that the nightmares disappeared. When you open the doors of your mind to toxic thinking, negativity, fear, atheism, or any other negative thing, your head will be infected. You need to close those doors and keep your mind clear.

FOUR: Speak undefeated. I will develop this topic more fully in Chapter Four, but let me say this now: you can't have a victorious mindset with a negative mouth. The way you speak affects the way you think. One of the most effective ways to change your thinking is to change your speaking. Stop saying, "Things won't work out," and start saying, "God is working all things together for my good." Don't say, "I can't trust anybody," say, "I will love others as God loves me." Instead of saying, "I don't look forward to tomorrow," say, "I'm excited for tomorrow because God has plans for good and not for evil, to give me a future and a hope." Your mouth affects your mindset.

One time, I was traveling through Mexico by bus, and our bus broke down in the city of Querétaro. We all had to disembark and wait for a replacement bus to arrive. It took forever. One fellow I spoke with had an extremely negative outlook. "Don't expect the replacement bus to be here until the morning. Just watch—this company is the worst. They won't even buy us a snack while we wait." His negativity rubbed off on me, and I began to speak my frustration to the other passengers around me.

There was one couple, however, that didn't share in our gloom. They were German tourists, and they were quite happy to wait for the replacement bus. They pulled snacks out of their backpacks and offered them to the other passengers while they answered questions about their homeland. Their cheerfulness was a rebuke to me. "I'm the Christian," I thought, "but instead of the joy of the Lord, I'm expressing nothing but misery." I walked over and sat down with the Germans. The first thing to change was my speech. Instead of speaking pessimism, I began to say things like, "I'm sure the bus will be here soon," and "At least it's a nice day to sit and talk."

That's when I noticed something remarkable. As I spoke life instead of death, my thinking changed. My mouth affected my mindset. I began to actually believe what I was speaking. I began to believe that God was going to work everything out for good. Just then, the bus driver called us over to the roadside store and offered to pay for our snack. He told us that the replacement bus would arrive in thirty minutes. "That wasn't so bad!" I said as we boarded the new bus a half hour later. Your mouth affects your mindset.

FIVE: Choose your circle. You need to choose your circle of friends carefully. If there are negative people in your inner circle, it will be much harder to live the undefeated life. A negative circle almost always produces a negative mind. You may have noticed that negative people love to spout off their opinion. Why are the unhappiest people the loudest? My advice is to challenge them. Don't let their negativity float around, infecting the environment. Bring the light of Christ into every dark situation. Be bold and speak life when their negativity hangs in the air. As you do this, the faith-filled people will be drawn to you, and the negative people will find some other room to infect. Just like one negative person can spoil an entire room, one positive person can transform an entire room with life and faith and hope.

My friend Wanda is like that. Whenever I ask her how she is doing, she answers, "I'm blessed." She is always giving and serving and making someone else's life a little better. Her positive spirit lifts the environment wherever she goes. One time I asked her why she is always so positive.

"My past was not very good," she said. "But when Jesus came into my situation with His salvation, I said, 'Lord, if you can save me from this mess, I will praise you with every single breath.' Well, He saved me, so I won't stop praising Him!" Find yourself a Wanda, and as much as possible, surround yourself with faith-filled, Jesus-centered, people-loving people like her. Their spirit will positively affect your mindset and make it much easier to change your thinking from defeated to victorious.

CHANGING your thinking is the first step to living the undefeated life. It doesn't matter how you grew up or how negative your thought patterns have been, you can change your thinking. Please know that I am praying for you as you read this book, that God will empower you to upgrade your thinking from defeated to undefeated.

Don't get discouraged if it's a difficult process. The mental castle of negativity that took you twenty years to build won't be torn down in one day. But take heart, it will be torn down. Keep coming back day after day and tear down one more brick. Before long, you will wake up and find that the old castle is gone. In its place, you will have built a new structure of healthy, positive, faith-filled thinking that will exert a positive influence on every area of your life.

Discussion Questions

1. Would you describe yourself as a generally-positive or generally-negative thinker?
2. Describe a time in your life when positive thinking brought positive results.
3. Read Philippians 4:8-9 and discuss how to apply these verses to your life.
4. Which of the Five Keys to Change Your Thinking do you find compelling, and why?
5. What is one area of negative thinking in your life that you identify and replace with God's truth this week?

2

A FAITH BIAS

"Words can never adequately convey the incredible impact of our attitude toward life. The longer I live the more convinced I become that life is 10 percent what happens to us and 90 percent how we respond to it. I believe the single most significant decision I can make on a day-to-day basis is my choice of attitude. It is more important than my past, my education, my bankroll, my successes or failures, fame or pain, what other people think of me or say about me, my circumstances, or my position. Attitude keeps me going or cripples my progress. It alone fuels my fire or assaults my hope. When my attitudes are right, there's no barrier too high, no valley too deep, no dream too extreme, no challenge too great for me."—Chuck Swindoll

"That's it. I'm done," I said. It was still eighty-five degrees at 5:00 PM in Ciudad Juarez, Mexico, and my attitude was not good. My wife Raquel and I were walking the crowded streets back to our hotel. We had spent the day in the American Consulate and received the news we didn't want to hear: there was a glitch in my wife's application for permanent residency in the United States. "Forget the whole thing. We can just live here in Mexico," I said. I was so frustrated with the delays and setbacks of the permanent residency process. I had assumed it would be easy for my Mexican-born wife to become an American citizen after we got married. It wasn't. It was long and grueling.

"Don't worry," Raquel said. "We'll find a way. We've come this far. I know God won't give up on us now!" Raquel always has a faith bias. She has the attitude of an overcomer. When confronted with a brick wall, she says, "I know there's a door here somewhere." I, on the other hand, sometimes struggle. There are times when I see nothing but bricks. This was one of those times. The whole walk back to the hotel, I grumbled and complained.

"I'm done," I said. "I wasn't planning on raising my kids in Mexico, but it is what it is. We will just stay here. I mean, I'm sad that my kids will never learn to surf in the Atlantic Ocean or see the great city of New York or go to a Yankees baseball game, but whatever." I was literally thinking about what bilingual school my children would attend when Raquel interrupted my thoughts.

"God's got this, honey," she said. When we arrived at the hotel, I reached into my pocket and pulled out the room key. With it came a business card that I'd forgotten about. The taxi driver had given it to us the night before, saying, "If you need any help, call Rosie." I didn't think much of it.

"That's it! Why don't we call Rosie?" Raquel said when she saw the business card in my hand. I wasn't in the mood for Rosie.

"Whatever," I said.

"It says she's an Immigration Lawyer. That's exactly what we need!" my wife said. I made the phone call, not expecting much. Rosie said to bring our paperwork to her office immediately. We made our way there, and within ten minutes Rosie had solved our problem. That was it—we were in the clear. As Raquel and I walked out of Rosie's office onto the humid streets again, I was able to breathe for the first time all day.

"I can't believe it was so simple! Thank you, Lord!" I said.

"I knew God would come through for us!" Raquel said. I learned a lesson that day that I've never forgotten. Your attitude makes all the difference in life. Raquel's attitude was positive and faith-filled, even in the face of an intimidating obstacle. My attitude was less than positive. If we had followed the direction my attitude was going, we wouldn't be living in America right now. The one thing I did right that day was listen to my wife's encouragement!

A Faith Bias

You need to have a faith bias in life. Every one of us faces daily challenges and setbacks. You can't choose to make them disappear. But you can choose to have the attitude of an overcomer in the midst of any difficulty. As leadership guru John Maxwell says, "God chooses what we go through, but we choose how we go through it."

Having a faith bias means you lean towards hope and faith and a positive mindset. You are predisposed to believe that God will, not God won't. You are on the faith team, not the doubt team. You trust that in every difficulty, God will make a way where there is no way. You know that even when things look bleak, God is still on the throne. You've learned that even when it's raining, there is sunshine behind the clouds. You are biased towards faith.

I know some people who have a *fail* bias. But they can't see it. Negative people rarely see themselves as negative. They think they have a realism bias. "I'm just being realistic. God has given me the gift of seeing the problems that can crop up." No, actually, Karen, you are just being negative. God has given you the gift of the Holy Spirit and the faith-filled Word of God, but you are not using them. You are choosing to look for the problem in every opportunity instead of finding the opportunity in every problem. You are biased towards failure.

There is only one way for you to get better. Take your fail bias and throw it into the sea. Get rid of it! Make a conscious choice from this day forward that you will choose to look for the ointment instead of the fly in the ointment. You will ask God to give you a faith bias.

The Power of Pre-Deciding

Before you leave the house in the morning, you need to put on your faith bias. Don't go out into the world without pre-deciding a few things:

1. **Whatever happens, God already knows.** Nothing takes God by surprise. Lots of things take us by surprise. But God is always in perfect, absolute, unruffled control. He never says, "Oh man, I forgot about that!" or "Oh boy, I didn't see that coming!" He always says, in every situation, "I've got a plan." Remind yourself of this every morning.
2. **For every challenge, God has a solution.** God has worked a solution into the design of every puzzle He creates. The solution is always there, even when we can't see it. Sometimes it's hidden, sometimes it's delayed, but it's always there. Trust the Solution Maker! If we could see the solution from the beginning, we wouldn't need God. He expects us to trust His ways and His timing. When we do, we always find the solution. Confess this over your life as you leave the house every day.
3. **God uses difficulties for His glory.** You are not going through trials randomly. God is using them to strengthen you and show the world His goodness and His glory. Your coworkers need to see that God answers prayer. Your friends need to see that God is real. Your neighbors need to see that your faith is not in vain. When God brings you out of your present difficulty, everyone else will see it and give glory to God.
4. **You will overcome through faith in His name.** Believe this, confess this, hold on to this. Don't leave the door with an attitude of doubt. If you do, you are pre-deciding on defeat. Instead, believe God for victory and insist upon it. Tell yourself, "Just like He has in the past, God is going to come

through for me today. I will face unexpected challenges, but they are no challenge for God. He will bring me out into a wide place, and everybody will see that God is with me and for me."

THAT'S what pre-deciding is all about. You are choosing to beat the devil to the punch and decide beforehand what you are going to believe. You don't wait for the trial to hit you and then think about how to react. That usually ends in failure, because our emotional response to pain is almost always negative. When you pre-decide to believe God and hold to His promises, the trial still hits you, but you are strong. You don't cave in to your emotions. You stand up and say, "God has something better coming. There is a solution here somewhere, and I'm excited to see how God is going to reveal it to me!"

Keep Believing

Recently my wife and I went on a date to New York City. We had a great day. We felt like kids again, just enjoying each other, the beautiful Fall weather, and the great city of New York. When we got back to the parking deck, I attempted to pay, but my card was declined.

"Uh oh," Raquel said. I pulled out my phone and checked our bank account balance. When I saw the figure, I let out a big sigh. "How much do we have in the account?" Raquel asked.

"You really want to know?" I said. "$8.59."

"Wait. Eighty or eight?"

"*Eight.*"

We both stood there shocked for a moment, and then paid with a different card and started walking to our car. We weren't down or depressed. We've been in this situation before, and we knew God had a solution. I remember that I had pre-decided that morning, before leaving the house, that whatever we might face, God was good and God was in control. As I walked back to the car, I prayed, "Alright God, here is your chance. Show us a way out and glorify your name!"

On the ride home, Raquel suddenly remembered something. "Oh my goodness!" she said. "Someone owes me $190. Let me text them right now, and I will pick up the check tomorrow." I too, had a flash of memory. I had never collected $250 from someone who owed me the money. I received it that very evening. The following day, I picked up an additional $600 check that was owed to me. So, in less than twenty-four hours, our bank account went from $8.59 to over one thousand dollars! I truly believe that Raquel's and my faith bias and our pre-decision to trust God impacted the outcome of the situation. We were determined to see the hand of God move, and we did.

Abraham's Faith Bias

The Biblical character Abraham had a faith bias. God had promised him that he would be the father of many nations, even though at the age of one hundred he still had no child. Abraham didn't freak out, though. His attitude was, "God will make a way." He would tell all his friends, "I'm going to be a grandfather."

"But . . . you don't have a child yet," they would say.

"That's coming," Abraham would reply. The Apostle Paul writes of Abraham,

> "In hope he believed against hope, that he should become the father of many nations, as he had been told, 'So shall your offspring be.' He did not weaken in faith when he considered his own body, which was as good as dead (since he was about a hundred years old), or when he considered the barrenness of Sarah's womb. No unbelief made him waver concerning the promise of God, but he grew strong in his faith as he gave glory to God, fully convinced that God was able to do what he had promised" (Rom. 4:18-21).

How can you be the father of many nations when you don't even have one son? You keep believing the promise of God, and watch Him work. Abraham's faith bias said, "I don't know how God is going to do it, but I am fully convinced that he will deliver on his promise to make me the father of many nations." And God did it. Abraham had Isaac, Isaac had Jacob, and Jacob had twelve sons who went on to become the heads of the twelve tribes of Israel. Abraham didn't feel the need to tell God how to do his job. He just felt the need to believe. This attitude of faith marked Abraham's life. It was his faith bias.

When God told him to leave his home country and launch out into the unknown, he had a faith bias. His attitude was, "Where God guides, God provides." And God did provide. God led him exactly where he needed to go. There were trials and challenges along the way (there always will be), but God fulfilled every promise he made to Abraham. How would you have reacted if God placed you in a situation like Abraham's? Would you have had a faith bias? I think many of us would have had a different kind of bias.

"Are you kidding me? Leave my place of comfort and go out there? What if I run out of money? What if my kids get sick? What if we get robbed? That's crazy talk!" This kind of thinking is a *fail* bias, and many of us respond to life this way. God calls us to new adventures, and we shrink back. God opens up new opportunities for us, and we make excuses. God asks us to believe big and we doubt bigger.

You Choose Your Bias

Every single day, you choose your bias. The overcomer chooses the bias of faith. It's an attitude. It's the lens through which you view life. When you face challenges, do you assume the worst, or do you assume that God has your back? The faith bias says, "It looks impossible, but God is able. There seems to be no way, but God will make a way. I seem to be out of options, but God always has something up his sleeve." The motto of the person of faith is, "But God!" When you face unsolvable riddles in your relationships, have a faith bias. God knows exactly how to work things out, if you let Him. When your finances are in crisis, listen to

God and do things His way. I promise you that He is the best financial advisor in the universe. When your health fails, believe in the Great Physician for a breakthrough. Healing may not come immediately, but it will come.

Don't be like my old friend Pete. Pete has the perpetual attitude of 'never enough.' If something good is happening, it's never good enough. If Pete has one blessing, he complains about not having two. His outlook can be summed up in two words, "Yeah but." Every time we talk on the phone, Pete tells me of some fresh trouble: his wife, his job, his health. So I spend thirty minutes building him up. I tell him to remember how good God is, that God has never let him down in the past and is not about to let him down this time, that things will surely get better.

After listening patiently to me, Pete responds. The words of his response vary, but the first two words never vary. They are always the same two words: "Yeah but." And with these two words, Pete dismantles everything I've told him for the past half hour. These two words, "Yeah but," undermine the promises of God and dig Pete deeper into his doubt and misery. I am convinced that Pete could live a happy and full life. He has a lot going for him. But he refuses to see the good. Don't be like Pete!

But God

What if you had a "But God" attitude instead of a "Yeah but" attitude? Family difficulty? But God's gonna help me through that. Job issues? But God's got good for me. Health challenges? But God is greater and He is my healer. You can train yourself to have a faith bias. Just like you learned to doubt and expect the worst, you can learn to trust and expect the best. Here's how you do it: the next time you doubt and think God will fail you, grab that thought and examine it.

"Hold up. God has never failed me in the past. Why am I thinking that everything will crash down this time?" Push back against your doubts and don't let them loiter in your head. I once read about a convenience store owner who struggled with unruly loiterers in front of his store. They were creating a mess and harassing customers. Nothing the store owner did could make them go away. Then one day, the store owner installed speakers outside his store. The first time he boomed classical music through his new speakers, the loiterers dispersed and never came back! My suggestion to you is to play a soundtrack in your head that the devil doesn't like. Put the promises of God on repeat!

"If God is for us, who can be against us?" (Rom. 8:31).

"No weapon that is fashioned against you shall succeed" (Isa. 54:17).

"And my God will supply every need of yours according to his riches in glory in Christ Jesus" (Phil. 4:19).

"All things are possible for one who believes" (Mark 9:23).

Your Day is Coming

Train yourself to have a faith bias. It will take discipline, especially at first, to push away the doubt and negativity that you have come to live with. But you can do it. God's Word will begin to root itself into your consciousness and a new, life-giving spirit will pervade your thinking. Instead of knee-jerk negativity, you will have knee-jerk faith.

I recently faced a challenge that tested my faith bias. Difficulties arose at the church I lead, and my first reaction was, "OK, let me pray about this. I'm sure God will clear this up right away." But He didn't. And instead of getting better, the problem got worse. It's easy to have a faith bias in life when God answers your prayers within twenty-four hours. It gets a bit more difficult when your problems persist for weeks, months and even years.

This particular problem persisted for years. I'm not going to lie, it's not easy to maintain a faith bias when your trouble sticks around that long. But God was teaching me an important lesson: God's delay is not God's denial. He had promised me in the very beginning of the trial that He was going to take care of everything, as long as I listened to Him and obeyed his Word. I did that, to the best of my ability, and still no breakthrough came.

But timing is God's job, not mine. His promises have the same power one year from now as they do today. I just needed to learn to wait. And in the waiting, I needed to learn to maintain my faith bias. I searched the Scriptures for five promises that spoke directly to the problem I was facing, and I memorized them. I highly recommend that you do the same. I began to repeat those five Scripture promises in the morning when I prayed, in the car as I drove, on the wooded trail as I ran. I decided it was not an option to give in to despair. What God had promised, He was going to deliver.

And then one day, He did it. Just like that. I don't know why He waited so long, but that doesn't matter, does it? God majestically, perfectly, exquisitely worked everything out for my good and His glory. I am still amazed at how He did it. All that is left for me to do is praise Him! You will probably have to maintain your faith bias for longer than you expect before your breakthrough comes. Don't give up! Keep listening to God and obeying his Word. Keep declaring His promises. Keep playing the soundtrack of faith in your head.

"And let us not grow weary of doing good, for in due season we will reap, if we do not give up" (Galatians 6:9).

Discussion Questions

1. Would you currently describe yourself as a person with a faith bias or a fail bias, and why?
2. Share one test of faith in your life that you passed, in other words, you made it through the difficulty with your faith intact and gave the glory to God.
3. Read Romans 4:18-21 and share how you can apply this passage to your own life.
4. What are some practical ways that you can build your faith and keep it fresh, so you will always respond to life's challenges with a faith bias?
5. Name one promise of God that you will hold on to this week when you face challenges to your faith.

3
UPGRADE YOUR MORNING

"The way you start your day determines how you live your day."—Robin Sharma

"And rising very early in the morning, while it was still dark, Jesus departed and went out to a desolate place, and there he prayed."—Mark 1:35

MAKE your habits and your habits make you. If you want to live undefeated and keep God first in your life, you will need to build godly habits into your life. Habits create consistency and keep you moving forward. Your most important habit, in my experience, is your first habit of the day: your time with God. Rising early to meet with God cleans out the cobwebs of yesterday and recharges you for the new day. If you get your morning right, you will get the whole day right.

"Oh my gosh, not again!" I dragged myself out of bed, ninety minutes past the time I had sworn to myself to rise the night before. "Why can't I do one simple thing: get out of bed?" I lamented. I was trying to revitalize my spiritual life, but I was stumbling before reaching the starting block. I had committed to a new regimen of early morning prayer and Bible study, but I kept failing at the 'early morning' part. "Maybe I will pray at night instead of in the morning. It's all the same to God, right?" I said.

There is nothing wrong with praying at night, but for me, it was a no. I found myself tired and distracted at night. There is something special about starting your day with God. There is something clarifying and edifying about making God's voice the first voice you hear in the morning, before the craziness of the day begins. There is a peace and a strength that are only found in the quiet, calm hours of the morning.

I struggled to establish a fixed habit of rising early in the morning. It was a protracted battle, but I finally succeeded in becoming an early riser. And once I did, my life changed. I was amazed, quite frankly, at the difference it made in my life. You too will be amazed at the difference it makes in your life when you upgrade your morning.

A Keystone Habit

Rising early to put God first in your day is what is known as a 'keystone habit.' Charles Duhigg, in his book, *The Power of Habit*, says that keystone habits are the most important habits to develop in your life, because they lead to the growth of other good habits.[1] Once I conquered the blankets and established my keystone habit of rising at 6:00 AM or earlier, other positive changes occurred in my life. I became far more productive, I greatly increased my output of studying and writing, and I lived with spiritual confidence because I was hearing from God every morning. Most importantly, I was honoring God's *law of firsts*. Whatever you put first is most important to you, and when you are faithful to put God first in your finances, in your time, or in your day, God will be faithful to bless you in return. When I got serious about putting God first in my day, God got serious about blessing my whole day.

When God led the children of Israel through the desert, He provided a miraculous food for them called manna. Every morning, the manna fell from heaven and fed the people. But the people had to gather the manna themselves. It didn't appear miraculously in their cupboards. They had to wake up, take their baskets and gather their own manna, or else they wouldn't eat that day. Here is the interesting thing: they had to gather the manna early in the morning. The Bible says that once the sun came out, the manna melted (Exo. 16:21). God had nourishment for them, but only if they rose early to get it. In the same way, God has spiritual nourishment for you, but only if you rise early to get it. He wants to speak to you, reassure you, guide you and fill you with faith and power in the morning.

Booth's Keystone Habit

In the 1880s a young man who loved Jesus got a job in a pawnshop in Nottingham, England. He didn't enjoy the work, but he worked hard until a better opportunity opened up. To prepare himself for a life of Christian service, he wrote on a scrap of paper the following resolutions: "I do promise God that I will rise early every morning to have a few minutes—not less than five—in private prayer... and I hereby vow to read no less than four chapters in God's Word every day."[2] That young man was William Booth. Booth went on to have a worldwide ministry that led thousands to Christ, and he later founded the Salvation Army, the Christian relief organization responsible for giving billions of dollars to alleviate suffering around the world since 1865. Booth's habit of rising early to meet with God was a keystone habit that marked his entire ministry. God saw Booth's faithfulness morning after morning and knew that He could trust him with greater influence and responsibility. Booth's success was due in part to his habit of meeting God in the morning.

Are you ready to upgrade your morning? It all starts with your morning routine. I have found that a well-crafted morning routine will get you pumped and promote your long-term success. You will look forward to waking up before anyone else is stirring. You will be tempted to post about it on social media and shout to the world, "I discovered an amazing secret that has changed my life!" I am going to share with you five key elements to a successful morning routine.

Five Key Elements of Your Morning Routine

ONE: Get up early. For me, this means at 6:00 AM or earlier. It's important that you rise before the busyness of the day so that you have uninterrupted time for prayer, reflection and Bible study. John Wesley rose at 4:00 in the morning to meet with God before the demands of the day confronted him. Benjamin Franklin famously said, "Early to bed and early to rise makes a man healthy, wealthy and wise." Thomas Jefferson said, "The sun has not caught me in bed in fifty years." Still today, many of the most successful people in the world get out of bed before 6:00 AM. It may require some adjustments for you to conquer the covers, but it's worth the sacrifice. Do whatever is necessary to give yourself some alone time every morning. Start by setting your alarm fifteen minutes earlier tomorrow. Once you do that successfully for a couple of days, subtract another fifteen minutes from your wake-up time. Keep doing this until you have a solid hour of alone time every morning. Trust me, this hour will become your favorite hour of the day. Once you feel the beauty of being refreshed and recharged in the presence of your loving Father, you will never allow the mattress to rob you again.

Pro tip for the drowsy: Years ago, I read an article about the benefits of cold water in the morning. The author said that a cold shower will instantly increase circulation and release endorphins that make you want to tackle the world. "Sounds crazy," I thought, "but I'm gonna try it." The first time I did, I woke my wife up with the screams. But I must admit, it worked. I left that shower wide awake and full of energy. I now use a modified cold-water method: I take my regular hot shower and then finish it with one full minute of cold water. Can I get a 'hallelujah' in this house? I assure you that the word 'drowsy' is no longer in my morning vocabulary.

. . .

TWO: Speak faith. The first thing out of your mouth in the morning should be faith, not fear or negativity. As soon as my feet hit the floor every morning, I speak my faith affirmations. You need to get the jump on things, before things get a jump on you. You need to let the world know, let your body know and let the devil know that you are going to have a good day, in Jesus' name. I speak something like this: "Thank you, Lord, for this day. Thank you that you have already conquered everything I will face today, and that you have already given me the victory through Jesus Christ. Thank you that you are in charge today, and as I submit to you, you are going to prosper me and use me, in Jesus' mighty name."

I learned this habit when I was in Bible College. We had a guest speaker who spoke about how he conquered his debilitating negative thoughts. He told of the time when he sank into depression, fear and hopelessness and was on the verge of giving up his preaching ministry. "How can I preach to others if I don't have the victory myself?" he said. Alone in his room, he flipped open his Bible. "Maybe God has something to say. I doubt it, but let's see if there is any hope in this book," he said.

His eyes fell on Joshua 1:8,

> "This Book of the Law shall not depart from your mouth, but you shall meditate on it day and night, so that you may be careful to do according to all that is written in it. For then you will make your way prosperous, and then you will have good success."

"I saw something in this verse I had never seen before," he said. "It says that this Book should not depart from your *mouth*. In other words, we are supposed to *speak* God's word, not just read it or hear it. Well, I had never done that before. Then I saw that my Bible had a margin note by the word 'meditate.' It said that the Hebrew word for 'meditate' means to 'utter, speak, muse, mutter.' I always thought that meditating referred to silent thinking. It never occurred to me that meditating involves speaking. But there it was, right in my Bible! I started to get fired up. Maybe this was the secret I'd been looking for! God is saying that I will have *good success* if I keep His words in my mouth, uttering them day and night. Wow!"

He recounted how he wrote Scripture verses on index cards and posted them all over his house. All day long, he would repeat what God says, counteracting his own negative thinking. Before long, his depression lifted, he got his mojo back, and instead of dropping out of the ministry, he stayed and continued to be faithful where God had planted him. Within one year, he was offered a dream job at a large church. All because he learned how meditate with his mouth!

His story impacted me. I went right to the college bookstore and purchased a package of index cards. I sat down in a sunny place, opened my Bible and began writing verses on the cards. I posted them all over my dorm room and started speaking them out loud every day. Thank God my roommate didn't mind!

I must say that since that time, Joshua 1:8 has become one of my favorite verses. Speaking God's Word has never failed me. Don't misunderstand. It's not magical, nor does it remove all pain and suffering from your life. But it does build your faith, spark your joy and elevate your peace in the midst of any storm you are facing. Speak God's Word first thing in the morning. Don't just let the day come at you—come at the day in the power that God has given you through Jesus Christ. Set the tone for the day before you take one step. You're the victor, not the victim. Speak the Word and set the tone!

THREE: Worship. I believe that worship is the heart of your morning routine. If you have to skip everything else, don't skip this step. Tune everything else out and spend time thanking, praising and worshipping God. Don't ask for anything, just worship. If you are still learning how to worship God, just keep it simple and tell God how much you love him. Don't worry, you will get more proficient with practice.

Worship is the most powerful force on the planet, because it brings God, the most powerful Being in the universe, into the room. Nothing attracts God quicker than true worship, since He is *seeking* those who worship him in spirit and in truth (John 4:23).

It was early one morning and I was out on the veranda of our hotel in the Dominican Republic. I was the leader of a group of teenagers on a missions trip. The sun was just coming up over the verdant landscape and the air was still cool. The melody of tropical birds mixed with the buzz of morning traffic to provide a soothing soundtrack for my morning devotions. With a cup of Dominican coffee in my hand, I was trying to pray. But I wasn't getting very far. My mind was weary and distracted. The harder I tried to pray, the more frustrated I got. Just then, from behind me, the strum of an acoustic guitar surprised me. One of the young men on our team had woken up early and brought his guitar up to the veranda. He began to sing that old chorus, "I Love You, Lord."

> *I love you, Lord*
> *And I lift my voice*
> *To worship You*
> *Oh, my soul rejoice!*
> *Take joy my King*
> *In what You hear*
> *Let it be a sweet, sweet sound in Your ear*[3]

I just sat and listened to him sing. With tears in my eyes, I realized something profound about worship that day. Worship is a love song. That's all it is. It can't be forced or programmed or plugged into a formula. Worship is simply love expressed. It's a dance of love, a sonnet of delight, a melody of praise. It's not complicated. I caught something on that veranda that has never left me. It's not hard to worship, because it's not hard to love. Especially when the Object of your love is perfect in every way. He is always faithful, always good, always better than you can imagine.

Just love God. That's worship. Worship God as part of your morning routine in the simplest and purest way possible. You might want to sing a song to him. Don't worry if you're not a good singer. You're not on *The Voice*. Just set your worship to music. Duncan Corby, Academic Dean of Hillsong College, writes about the connection between music and worship:

> "As believers, we love the Lord with all our heart, soul, mind and strength. And music uniquely has the power to engage the entirety of who I am in that moment of expressing my devotion to God. When I sing in worship I am engaged emotionally, physically and intellectually. It's like 'all of me' is caught up in this act of love. It's music that makes this happen. . . . I pour myself out in a song of worship, and feel that I'm finally able to get close to expressing all that is in my heart to say, but for which mere spoken words seem insufficient."[4]

FOUR: Read your Bible and pray. I place these two activities together, because as part of my morning routine, I prayerfully read my Bible and then I Biblically pray. This is my time for devotional reading of the Bible, not deeper Bible study. I open the Word and ask, "What is God saying to me this morning?" not "What is the historical and exegetical interpretation of the beast in Revelation 6?" or "What verse can I use in Point 3 of this week's sermon?"

More often than not, God will speak to me through His Word. What do I mean, "God will speak to me"? I don't mean that I hear an audible voice. I mean that God will speak something directly relevant to my life through the pages of Scripture. It's uncanny. I might be reading an Old Testament story I've read many times before and bam! all of a sudden, I see a new insight that applies perfectly to the situation I am currently facing. How does God do that? I don't know, but I do know that the Bible is like no other book.

George Müller, the great English evangelist from the 1800's, realized that he had been praying wrongly for years. Previously, he woke up and went straight to prayer. He often found himself frustrated after half an hour, unable to break through in prayer. Then, he discovered the secret of going to the Word before he went to prayer.

> "The point is this: I saw more clearly than ever, that the first great and primary business to which I ought to attend every day was, to have my soul happy in the Lord. The first thing to be concerned about was not, how much I might serve the Lord, how I might glorify the Lord; but how I might get my soul into a happy state, and how my inner man might be nourished. . . . The first thing I did, after having asked in a few words the Lord's blessing upon His precious Word, was to begin to meditate on the Word of God; searching, as it were, into every verse, to get blessing out of it; not for the sake of the public ministry of the Word; not for the sake of preaching on what I had meditated upon; but for the sake of obtaining food for my own soul. The result I have found to be almost invariably this, that after a very few minutes my soul has been led to confession, or to thanksgiving, or to intercession, or to supplication; so that though I did not, as it were, give to prayer but to meditation, yet it turned almost immediately more or less to prayer."[5]

The secret is to read the Word and pray the Word. First let the Word encourage you and fill your soul, then pray as the Word leads you. My favorite portions of Scripture to use in this way are the Psalms and the Gospels. The Psalms are particularly suited to prayer, and the words of Jesus never lose their power.

FIVE: Daily list. After you finish reading your Bible and praying, you are not done with your morning routine yet. The Bible says, "The plans of the diligent lead surely to abundance, but everyone who is hasty comes only to poverty" (Prov. 21:5). If you fail to plan, you plan to fail. God is a God of order, and he expects us to plan our days. Paul said that all things should be done "decently and in order" (1 Cor. 14:40), and

Jesus asks the question, "For which of you, desiring to build a tower, does not first sit down and count the cost, whether he has enough to complete it?" (Luke 14:28). This speaks of careful planning.

For me, the best way to plan is to write a list every morning based on my previously-set priorities. I don't write a random list of to-dos. I write my list on a grid of priorities, scaled from most important to least important. That way, I never get bogged down doing tasks that are important but low priority. I always tackle my top-priority tasks first. For example, every week I am responsible for bringing a fresh and powerful sermon to my congregation. This is a high-priority task. Other tasks must get downgraded on my list until this task is completed (usually by Tuesday evening). If I get caught up in lower-priority tasks and don't finish my sermon preparation until Saturday night, I am cheating my congregation.

This is why I am such a believer in writing a daily list of priority tasks. Every morning, ask yourself, "What is the most important thing I must accomplish today? What one thing will bring the most value to my business, or my family, or my personal development? What task, if left undone, would bring the most harm to my business, or my family, or my personal development?" That is your number-one task. Then, ask yourself, "What is the second most important thing I must accomplish today?" and so on. I carry my list with me on my phone and check it throughout the day. Once you catch the power of following a prioritized daily list, you will never live another day without one.

SIX: (BONUS) Eat your frog. I said that I was going to give you five key elements of a morning routine, but here is a free bonus. The last thing you should do before breakfast is to eat your frog. It might sound strange, but this is one of the most powerful principles in life. Brian Tracy, in his book *Eat That Frog!*, clarifies this concept.

> "It has been said that if the first thing you do each morning is to eat a live frog, you can go through the day with the satisfaction of knowing

that that is probably the worst thing that is going to happen to you all day long. Your 'frog' is your biggest, most important task, the one you are most likely to procrastinate on if you don't do something about it. It is also the one task that can have the greatest positive impact on your life and results at the moment."[6]

I find this to be great advice, and it's something I try to live by. First thing in the morning, eat your frog. Don't think too much about it; train yourself to jump in and tackle your biggest task first. Is it a difficult phone call you need to make or an email you need to write? Is it a project you need to finalize or a decision you need to make? Do it early, and the rest of your day will be easier. If you wait, chances are that it will never get done. If you eat your frog before breakfast, you will enter the day confidant and ready to do good for the world.

I HAVE USED this morning routine with great success for years. Most of this book, in fact, was written in the early morning hours, before my other pastoral and familial duties of the day began. What does your morning routine look like? Take some time today, sit down with a pen and paper and draft a morning routine for yourself. You will probably tweak it over time, but you need to start somewhere. Before long, your morning routine will become precious to you. Once you drink the delights of the river of God in the early morning, you will never give preference to your pillows again. The morning will become your favorite time of the day.

Discussion Questions

1. Do you consider yourself a morning person or a night owl?
2. Describe your current morning routine.

3. Which of the Five Key Elements of Your Morning Routine spoke to you the most, and why?
4. Explain how your life would change for the better if you spent quality time with God every morning.
5. What is the most impactful change you could make to your morning routine, starting tomorrow?

4
SPEAK LIFE

"When a man is filled with the Word of God you cannot keep him still. If a man has got the Word, he must speak or die."—Dwight L. Moody

"Ugh, I hate this job," I said to wife. "It sucks the life out of you and leaves you cold, dead and abandoned on the floor."

After a pause, she said, "A little dramatic, perhaps?"

"Not at all," I insisted.

"I'm sorry, honey," she said, "but I know God will provide something better soon."

"Yeah, but when, oh God?" I thought.

It was the early 2000's and I was working at a job that I didn't want to work at. But I needed the money. I had a wife and two young kids to support, so I went to work every day. But I didn't go happily. I went unhappily, and I let others know about it. "What do I do for a living? Well, I currently manage the office in the fifth circle of hell. How about you? . . . My job? It's great. If by 'great' you mean torturous, mind-numbing, soul-sucking and generally loathsome."

I didn't realize the power of my words at the time. My habit of speaking discontent, unbelief and negativity had one result: it increased my discontent, unbelief and negativity. Instead of making me better, my mouth was making me bitter. I needed an intervention, and God brought it to me by way of the Biblical character King David.

David Speaks Life

David was only sixteen or seventeen, but he had already learned one of the greatest secrets to living the undefeated life. David knew how to speak life. The story is found in 1 Samuel 17, and it's one you might be familiar with. Two armies faced each other in a standoff, the Israelites versus the Philistines. The best warrior from one army was to come forward and fight a duel with the best warrior from the other army. Winner take all. The only problem was, no one wanted to fight Goliath, the Philistine warrior, because he was big. Really big. Nine-stinking-feet tall and never lost a battle.

All the soldiers on the Israelite side were speaking defeat and unbelief. "We're as good as dead. Did you see the size of that guy? I could never fight him!" I'm quite sure their mouths were making them miserable. David came on the scene and was genuinely shocked by the unbelief and negativity he was hearing. He was offended that Goliath mocked the God of Israel and no one was willing to stand up and do something about it.

"Really, guys? No one will step up and fight Goliath? OK then, I'll just do it myself!" David said.

They brought David to King Saul. When Saul expressed doubt in David's ability, considering his age and inexperience, David boldly declared, "Your servant used to keep sheep for his father. And when there came a lion, or a bear, and took a lamb from the flock, I went after him and struck him and delivered it out of his mouth. And if he arose against me, I caught him by his beard and struck him and killed him. Your servant has struck down both lions and bears, and this uncircumcised Philistine shall be like one of them, for he has defied the armies of the living God" (1 Sam. 17:34-36).

David spoke faith. He didn't say, "Maybe Goliath will fall." He declared, "Goliath *will* fall." He didn't look at the negatives—he declared the positives. David was in the habit of speaking life. Your speech patterns are a habit, and you can develop the habit of speaking life. David spoke faith and life. Everyone around him spoke death and defeat. "Goliath is too big. We might as well surrender." But that didn't bother David. If you are going to develop the habit of speaking life, please know that negative talk will surround you. Negative talkers are everywhere. Don't let their negativity rub off on you—just keep speaking life.

David declared, "I will take care of Goliath myself."

They said, "But you are only seventeen!" David said, "I'm old enough to kill a lion and a bear."

They said, "But you don't have any armor." David said, "I can hurl a mean stone."

They said, "Goliath has never lost a battle." David said, "Well, he's about to lose his first one. And his head will look real nice on my mantelpiece."

The Doubters Will Test You

Just like David, you will be tested when you begin to speak life into a situation. If you say, "I am believing God for a healing," they will say, "Yes, but God doesn't heal everybody." If you say, "God is going to bless me financially," they will say, "I believed that once and it didn't work." If you say, "We are trusting the Lord to bring our prodigal son back home," they will say, "Well, mine is thirty-nine and he's still an atheist." People who have given up on their dreams love to trample on yours. Don't let them. Immerse yourself in God's Word and arm yourself with His promises, and keep speaking life.

When my wife was pregnant with our fourth child, we received the phone call from her doctor that no one wants to receive. "Mr. and Mrs. Murphy?" he said.

"Yes?" we answered as we put him on speakerphone.

"I'm afraid I have some bad news about Raquel's pregnancy," he said. There was a pause and then he said, "The placenta is fifty percent separated from the wall of the uterus."

"Is that bad?" we asked.

"Yes," he replied gravely. "Very bad. Mr. and Mrs. Murphy, I would prepare to lose this baby." Time stood still as we remained motionless with my wife's cell phone in our hands, unable to reply.

"Um thank you, doctor," we finally managed, and hung up. My wife and I reacted as we always react to life's unexpected twists: we immediately brought it to God. We weren't going to dwell on what man says. We wanted to know what God says. After spending time seeking the Lord, both of us agreed that the baby was going to live. How did we know? God, through his Holy Spirit, had spoken to our hearts in prayer. He gave us peace and assurance and faith. We had walked with God long enough to know that if God was giving us faith in prayer, it was a good sign that the baby was going to live.

Speaking What We Believe

So we began to speak life. Of course, we knew there was a chance that we could lose the baby, and if that had happened, we would get through it. But we had faith for life, so we spoke our faith out loud every chance we got. "We believe the baby is going to live," we said to our friends and relatives. "This is just a momentary challenge. God is with us, and His blessing is on this child." It didn't take long for the doubters to test us.

"I don't know why you think that," some of them said. "The doctor said that you will either lose the baby or it will be born disabled." The doctor never said that last part, but you know the devil likes to speak death, even if he has to make up falsehoods. Their words stung momentarily, but we stood our ground.

"God has given us assurance and faith, and that is what we are standing on." You will have to do the same thing when you step out and speak life into your situation. There will be at least one doubter who thinks their mission is to bring you back down to reality. Don't be intimidated by them. Keep speaking life.

The good news is that Raquel's pregnancy went full term with no further complications, and on November 13, 2008, one of the happiest days of my life, my beautiful, perfectly-healthy baby Brianna was born. She brings joy to my life every single day. Can I get a 'hallelujah' in this house? God always has the last word. And in this case, it was, "Life!"

Small Wins Lead to Greater Victories

Returning to our story of David and Goliath, we see David speaking faith in the presence of doubters. Where did David get this faith? The answer comes from the sheepfold. As a shepherd, David won small but significant victories. David was sure he could win against Goliath because God had given him victories in the past. His smaller victories as a shepherd gave him faith for his biggest battle yet. Your past victories always increase your faith for future battles. Every time you pray and God answers, your faith increases. Every time God delivers you from trouble, your faith increases. Every time God provides for you in the nick of time, your faith increases. Today's victories, however small, are preparing you for tomorrow's battles. David had confidence to speak life into the Goliath situation because God had given him victory over the lion and the bear in the past. And here's the cool thing: every time David spoke faith, his faith increased. It tends to work that way. When you speak faith, your faith increases. When you speak doubt, your doubt increases. Your mouth has amazing power to strengthen or weaken your own courage, to embolden or debilitate your own faith, to inspire or impede your own action. What you speak invariably moves you in one direction or another. When David spoke his faith to King Saul, David's faith increased.

Speaking Faith in the Battle

King Saul saw the faith of young David and released him to fight Goliath. The duel was drawn up. When David stood there alone, facing his massive, armor-clad opponent, he had one more chance to use his mouth to either declare victory or admit defeat. No one would have faulted him if he had said, "You know what? On second thought, I'm going to pass on this one. I'm not feeling 100% today, so I think I'd better sit this one out. Maybe next week."

But that's not what David said. David was ready to boldly declare his faith. Even though it was impossible. Even though others doubted. Even though his own army hid in fear. David had faith, even if he had to have faith alone. He knew his God was was bigger than Goliath. And he knew his God was with him. David stood up, squared his shoulders and shouted,

"You come to me with a sword and with a spear and with a javelin, but I come to you in the name of the Lord of hosts, the God of the armies of Israel, whom you have defied. This day the Lord will deliver you into my hand, and I will strike you down and cut off your head" (1 Sam. 17:45-46).

And that is exactly what happened! God honored David's bold confession of faith and Goliath fell. David's career as Israel's greatest king was launched that day. And it all started because David knew how to speak life.

What I Learned From David

The story of David defeating Goliath was exactly what I needed to shake me out of my negative malaise over the undesirable job I mentioned at the beginning of this chapter. I saw that I needed to speak life into my situation. I realized that my negative words were actually harming my faith. So, I decided to make a change. I went to prayer and asked God to speak to me about my future. God reminded me that my calling is to be a pastor and a leader, that my destiny is to change the world through the power of God's Word, that great things were to come if I would just believe. "Yes, Lord, I believe," I prayed. "I don't see any of those things with my eyes, but I will begin to speak my faith publicly and let you promote me when you see fit."

I began to tell people that my calling was to be a pastor and that my current job was a just a temporary assignment. I felt a shift take place. Nothing at my job had changed, but something had changed inside of me. My new boldness in speaking my faith sparked an increase in the very faith I was speaking about. My words had power. Each time I told someone about my future calling in God, I became more sure that God had great things for me. Your mouth can build your faith!

Within a couple of weeks after changing my speech from negative to faith-filled, I got a job offer. I wasn't looking for a job in this particular organization, because I didn't think they were hiring. Not only were they hiring, but they were looking for someone with my exact credentials. Needless to say, I didn't have to think twice about accepting this new job offer. I was hired and worked there as a pastor, teacher and counselor for a decade. It was an amazing opportunity that honed my skills for my current position as the lead pastor of a church. What did I learn from this experience? God honors faith, and faith is built up when you speak it out of your mouth. Your words have power.

What Words Can't Do

Now, let me clarify what your words do *not* have the power to do. Due to erroneous teaching in certain circles, some think that your words have the power to create reality, make you wealthy and remove suffering from your life. This is misleading at best.

Your words can create a new inner reality, to the extent that they change your thinking, but they don't create your outer reality. Only God can do that. Instead of chanting mantras to create your outer reality, just submit to a good and loving Father and ask Him to do it. He will always work all things together for your good and His glory.

Words alone cannot make you wealthy. To increase wealth, you must follow God's financial principles, which include giving God your first ten percent, conducting your financial matters with integrity, working diligently, avoiding debt and saving a significant portion of your income. I know it sounds more fun to shout at your wallet, "Be filled!" but it doesn't work. So, please don't. God is not a genie in a bottle and can't be manipulated that way. Submit to His goodness. He will care for you and provide for your needs.

And words will not remove all suffering from your life. They can certainly make a difficult situation better by injecting faith into it, but they can't remove the difficulty altogether. Struggles and difficulties are part of God's good plan for our lives. They make us stronger, they give us perspective, they make us long for heaven, and they make us more compassionate on others who suffer.

Words Have Power

Words have power. I don't want to diminish this powerful truth by mentioning these cautions. As long as we don't go to extremes, it is perfectly legitimate to use the power of words to build faith and create a positive, life-giving atmosphere.

The Apostle Paul knew how to speak life into his situation. He wrote, "It is written: 'I believed; therefore I have spoken.' Since we have that same spirit of faith, we also believe and therefore speak" (2 Cor. 4:13 NIV). Paul was saying, "If you believe it, speak it." He was referring primarily to faith in the Gospel of Jesus Christ, but I think this verse also applies to other areas of the Christian life. Speak life, even when others don't believe. If God has given you faith, speak it out, and He will honor you. You may be facing an impossible situation. I encourage you to speak life and watch God do the impossible.

Speak Life into Impossible Circumstances

My friends Vinnie and Maria know what it's like to stare impossibility in the face and come out winning. In 2010, they received a devastating doctor's report. After giving birth at age thirty-eight, Maria was told that she had Post-Partum Cardiomyopathy. Her heart was only functioning at 10% capacity, and her lungs and kidneys were shutting down. The doctors sent her home with a literal death sentence. In most cases, that would be the end of the story. In this case, however, Vinnie and Maria went to prayer, and God encouraged them to believe for life. So they did. They fought against the darkness and depression and began to speak life.

I ran into Vinnie not long after they received the diagnosis and asked him how things were going. "Well, we received a bad report from the doctor, Pastor Dave, but we are believing God for a total healing," he said.

"Total healing!" I said. "I am so encouraged by your strong faith, Vinnie. How do you stay positive?"

"I've learned that you have to feed your faith and speak your faith. I have a list of twenty-five healing Scriptures that I repeat out loud every day as I pace the floors in my home, praying," Vinnie said.

"Wow," I said. "Twenty-five Scriptures. And you declare them out loud every day?"

"Yes," replied Vinnie. "That is our conviction from the Lord. We just believe that if we are faithful to declare His Word, He will be faithful to send the healing in His time."

"Give me some examples of the verses that you declare," I said.

Vinnie answered, "Some of my favorite verses are,

Exodus 15:26, 'If you will diligently listen to the voice of the Lord your God, and do that which is right in his eyes, and give ear to his commandments and keep all his statutes, I will put none of the diseases on you that I put on the Egyptians, for I am the Lord, your healer.'

Isaiah 53:5, 'But he was pierced for our transgressions; he was crushed for our iniquities; upon him was the chastisement that brought us peace, and with his wounds we are healed.'

James 5:15, 'And the prayer of faith will save the one who is sick, and the Lord will raise him up.'"

Maria's healing did not come quickly. Weeks and then months

passed with no improvement. But Vinnie and Maria stood in faith and boldly declared, "We are believing God for total healing." They didn't hide their faith, they confessed it with their mouths. When the setbacks came, they stood in faith. When Maria's progress seemed to go backward, they stood in faith. Finally, one October morning, the phone rang. "It's the doctor," Maria whispered to Vinnie as she called him to the phone.

"I have some good news," the doctor said.

"Yes?" Vinnie and Maria answered in unison.

"Well, your latest test results look good. Really good. I don't understand it, to be honest. This is certainly out of the ordinary. But you said you wanted a miracle—it looks like you got it. Maria's heart is functioning normally!"

What is the miracle that you are standing in faith for? Keep speaking life and believing God for great things. Don't be swayed by the doubters. Take God at His Word and don't let His Word depart from your mouth. In due season, God will come through for you.

Your Miracle is Coming

When you face an impossible situation and God tells you to trust Him, trust Him with your mouth. Speak your faith. Don't hold it in. Tell others that your God is bigger than your impossibility, and He loves you too much to let you go. Your miracle is coming, just keep believing and confessing life. Very often, it's a test. Will you confess Him before men, or will you cave in to your doubts? In my second year of Bible college, I realized that I didn't have enough money to pay the tuition for the next semester. I knew that God had sent me there, and every time I prayed about it, I felt that God was telling me to move forward in faith. Part of me wanted to say, "But that won't pay the bills, God!" (remember, I'm from New Jersey), but I controlled myself and did my best to speak life. "God will come through for me," I told my friends. "He has never let me down before, and I know He won't let me down now."

As the deadline drew near, my faith was stretched thinner, but it never broke. "I know you are going to do something, God. I don't have the money, but I know you do!" Two days before the deadline, I stopped by the school finance office. I was going to ask for a payment plan or a loan.

"For which semester, Mr. Murphy?" the woman asked me.

"For the upcoming semester," I answered.

"Well, it says here that your upcoming semester is paid in full," she said.

"Uh, come again?" I asked.

"That's right. A donor who wishes to remain anonymous deposited the full amount into your account last Tuesday."

"Oh my goodness, I don't know what to say. Thank you!" I said as I ran outside and shouted into the Texas sun, "Hallelujah!" When God gives you assurance in prayer, believe it and speak it. That's your part. God's part, and He does it well, is to bring the miracle at just the right time!

Discussion Questions

1. If everything you said was recorded for one week, would the person listening to the recording say you have a strong faith or a weak faith?
2. When your faith is tested, do you tend to complain or do you have the discipline to keep speaking life?
3. What Scripture passages can you name that teach us to speak life? Explain them to the group or to the person next to you.
4. How would your life be different if you never complained again, and only spoke faith in the midst of your challenges?
5. What is one area in which you need to change your speech from negative to positive, starting today?

5

DISCOVER PRAISE

"When you praise God, you destroy the obstacles Satan puts in your way. Praise sets you up for a miracle!"—Terry Law

HAVE you discovered the power of praise? In my thirty years of walking with Jesus, I've not found anything as powerful as praise. Before you say, "I'm not a good singer," please understand that praise has more to do with your heart than your melody. God delights in your praises, whether you sing like an angel or croak like a frog. Praise is the soundtrack of the undefeated life, and you should turn it up!

I woke up to the sound of Cesar praising Jesus. "Hallelujah, thank you, Lord, that you are with me today! Thank you that you control all things in your sovereign goodness. I bless your beautiful name, Lord." It was 1993, and Cesar and I had spent the night in the rustic dorm of a church in Queens, New York. We were doing homeless outreach ministry on a frigid weekend in December. I had met Cesar the night before and learned that he was a New York native who regularly engaged in homeless ministry. We ended up randomly assigned to the same dorm room. Breakfast was at 8:00, but I looked at my watch and saw that it was only 6:30.

"Hey Cesar, you're up early," I said.

"Just praising His name, Dave," he replied.

At breakfast, I asked Cesar a question. "Hey man, I noticed that you praise Jesus nonstop. I think that's awesome, but how do you keep it going all the time?"

"Keep it going?" he said. "I can't stop it. Jesus saved me and filled me with his Holy Spirit and this is just the outflow of that blessing. The Bible says the rocks will cry out of I don't praise Him, so I'm gonna keep praising Him.

"Now, what you might not know about me is that I used to be homeless myself. I was down and I was out, you know what I'm saying? My life was a mess, and I was mad at God for allowing me to get into that mess. I didn't want anything to do with God or church, but there was this one annoying pastor who wouldn't stop reaching out to me and loving me and inviting me to his church. He would buy me hot coffee and make sure I had a warm bed in the wintertime.

"Finally, on a freezing cold weekend, like this one, I dragged myself to his church just to keep warm. I stood in the back because I didn't want anyone seeing me. They had a huge choir, and when they started singing, well, I'd never heard anything like that in my life. I stood there and cried the whole service. At the end, the pastor saw me and called me to come down to the front of the church. I went down there and gave my life to Jesus. I felt something lift off of me that day. I knew something had changed. That church got me into their Christian rehab program and my life has never been the same. So, why do I praise Jesus all the time? My answer is, how can I not praise Him? After all He did for me, the least I can do is thank Him!"

The Secret of Praise

You might not have a background as gritty as Cesar's, but learn this one lesson from his life: praise is the soundtrack of the undefeated life. The

Bible says, "Praise the Lord" almost 250 times. The sounds of praise should fill our hearts and fill our homes. Cesar and I became friends and keep in touch since that weekend, and I have never seen him lose his victory or his praise. Is it a coincidence that the happiest and most victorious people are the ones who praise the most? I don't think so. They have the same problems we have, but they have learned the secret of praising God to keep their faith fresh and strong. Praise is the strength of the people of God, and it's one of the greatest keys to living the undefeated life. If you don't know how to praise, get excited, because it's easy to learn!

Praising God in the Valley

Praise has gotten me through the deepest valleys of my life. We know that God is good, but there are times when it doesn't feel like it. There are seasons when we say, "God, I know it's great up there in heaven, but down here on earth, it's pretty sucky." Praise is the bridge between heaven and earth. If you want to experience a bit of heaven on earth, learn to praise.

I woke up one morning with a heaviness and a dread. Not a great start to my Monday. Before I got out of bed, I was battling a dark cloud of worry, fear and anxiety. There were issues in my life, beyond my control, that were really weighing me down. I dragged myself downstairs and sank into my prayer seat. I tried to pray, but not much prayer was coming out. It was like trying to water the lawn with a kink in the hose. Prayer was just dribbling out.

The fact is, I had already prayed about the issues that were weighing me down. In my funk, I was thought, "How many times do I have to repeat the same prayer?" I picked up my Bible for some inspiration. I stared at the cover for a minute or two and gave up. I had nothing.

This prayer time was on its way to be one of my all-time worst. Thankfully, I knew a secret that saved me before my entire morning was a total fail. This is a secret I learned a long time ago, and it has virtually never failed me. I got up from my seat and started to pace the floor. I began to thank and praise the Lord. Every time a thought or a worry or even a prayer request came to my mind, I pushed it away and kept praising. My prayer time had become a praise time. The secret I had learned is this: *when you can't pray, praise.*

When You Can't Pray, Praise

I paced the floor and kept thanking and praising God. Before long, a ray of light entered my soul. Just ten minutes before, my soul was heavy and dark. Now, in the presence of the living God, my soul was bathed in light. I knew something. I knew that God was good. I knew that God loved me. And I knew that God had heard my prayers. In that moment, I felt like there was not much more that I needed to know. I literally felt lighter and began to praise God a little louder. My pace quickened and my hands lifted up to heaven. The hose was unkinked and the praise was flowing.

"Bless the Lord, O my soul," I said, "and all that is within me, bless his holy name!" (Psalm 103:1). I had faith now. Nothing had changed in my situation, but something had changed in me. My troubles were the same, but my soul was different. "Jesus, you are the miracle worker," I said, "and nothing can stop your hand. Move mightily, Lord! I trust you to do it, and I believe it's done, in Jesus' name." About two weeks after this prayer, I saw a distinct shift in my situation. God was doing what no man can do. He was moving mountains like only He can do. The entire miracle took many months to be completed, but I believe a significant shift took place that morning in my praise time. That's where the breakthrough was achieved—it just took some time to be worked out in the natural.

How crazy that what started out as one of my worst prayer times ended up being one of my best. Praise took it from worst to first. Can I encourage you? The next time you find it difficult to pray, drop everything and praise. Don't ask God for anything, don't get distracted, just praise. I promise you that your breakthrough will come.

Start Simply

It you find it difficult to praise, start simply. Grab a Bible, open to Psalm 145 and read it out loud as a praise to the Lord. Psalm 145 is one of those Bible passages that can pull you out of a hole and put you in a happy place again. It's filled with awesome reminders of God's goodness and faithfulness, plus His tender and personal care of you. It would be a great idea for you to read this Psalm out loud every morning. How about we start right now? Below is the entire text of Psalm 145. I encourage you to read it as a praise offering to the Lord, and watch how your faith is strengthened, your spirit is lifted and your heart is renewed!

> 1 I will exalt you, my God the King;
> I will praise your name for ever and ever.
> 2 Every day I will praise you
> and extol your name for ever and ever.
> 3 Great is the Lord and most worthy of praise;
> his greatness no one can fathom.
> 4 One generation commends your works to another;
> they tell of your mighty acts.
> 5 They speak of the glorious splendor of your majesty—
> and I will meditate on your wonderful works.
> 6 They tell of the power of your awesome works—
> and I will proclaim your great deeds.
> 7 They celebrate your abundant goodness
> and joyfully sing of your righteousness.
> 8 The Lord is gracious and compassionate,
> slow to anger and rich in love.
> 9 The Lord is good to all;
> he has compassion on all he has made.
> 10 All your works praise you, Lord;
> your faithful people extol you.

11 They tell of the glory of your kingdom
and speak of your might,
12 so that all people may know of your mighty acts
and the glorious splendor of your kingdom.
13 Your kingdom is an everlasting kingdom,
and your dominion endures through all generations.
The Lord is trustworthy in all he promises
and faithful in all he does.
14 The Lord upholds all who fall
and lifts up all who are bowed down.
15 The eyes of all look to you,
and you give them their food at the proper time.
16 You open your hand
and satisfy the desires of every living thing.
17 The Lord is righteous in all his ways
and faithful in all he does.
18 The Lord is near to all who call on him,
to all who call on him in truth.
19 He fulfills the desires of those who fear him;
he hears their cry and saves them.
20 The Lord watches over all who love him,
but all the wicked he will destroy.
21 My mouth will speak in praise of the Lord.
Let every creature praise his holy name
for ever and ever.

Old School is the Good School

Another simple way to start praising is to get a hymn book and learn a few songs. Years ago, I bought a hymn book to use in my personal prayer times, and it has become precious to me. I have never been a member of church that sings hymns, but I have always loved the old songs. They have a depth, a power and a permanency that is sometimes missing today. I have experienced many winter mornings where nothing but an old hymn could awaken my soul. One of my favorites is "Jesus Paid It All." (If you don't know the melody, just look it up online.)

Jesus Paid It All
VERSE 1
I hear the Savior say,
"Thy strength indeed is small.
Child of weakness, watch and pray,
Find in Me thine all in all."
REFRAIN
Jesus paid it all, all to Him I owe;
Sin had left a crimson stain,
He washed it white as snow.
VERSE 2
Lord, now indeed I find
Thy pow'r, and Thine alone,
Can change the leper's spots
And melt the heart of stone.
VERSE 3
For nothing good have I
Whereby Thy grace to claim;
I'll wash my garments white
In the blood of Calv'ry's Lamb.
VERSE 4
And when, before the throne,
I stand in Him complete,
"Jesus died my soul to save,"
My lips shall still repeat.[1]

New School is Cool

Thank God for the old hymns, but don't limit yourself to the old. There is a lot of great modern worship that is full of depth, power and anointing. My life has been changed and my days have been filled by the sounds of modern worship. We have unprecedented access to this phenomenal worship via streaming services like Spotify. My iPhone is now a source of endless praise. One of my current favorites is Elevation Worship's "Do It Again." It has been an absolute breath of fresh air to me lately!

Do It Again
VERSE 1
Walking around these walls
I thought by now they'd fall
But You have never failed me yet
Waiting for change to come
Knowing the battle's won
For You have never failed me yet
REFRAIN
Your promise still stands
Great is Your faithfulness, faithfulness
I'm still in Your hands
This is my confidence, You've never failed me yet
VERSE 2
I know the night won't last
Your Word will come to pass
My heart will sing Your praise again
Jesus, You're still enough
Keep me within Your love
My heart will sing Your praise again
BRIDGE
I've seen You move, come move the mountains
And I believe, I'll see You do it again
You made a way, where there was no way
And I believe, I'll see You do it again[2]

I Can't Sing

The other day I was at my local running trail, and as I was preparing to run, a woman walked by, singing loudly. She had large headphones on her head, and either she didn't notice or didn't care that she sounded like a frog. A dying frog. A dying frog being slowly tortured to death. At first, I thought, "Oh sweet Jesus." But then it occurred to me, "I wish more Christians were so bold to sing and praise Jesus in public!"

There is no excuse not to praise God. You might say, "I can't sing." Well, neither can I. But that hasn't stopped me from praising God for the last thirty years. Praising God has nothing to do with musical ability —it has to do with heart ability. When your heart is in it, God doesn't care what the tune sounds like. What sounds sweet to Him is faith. Don't let the devil steal your praise because you are self-conscious about your singing ability. Lift your song to the Lord, put your whole heart into it, and God will say, "Sounds perfect to me." The next time you are alone in your car, in your place of prayer, in the shower, I challenge you to sing a song to Jesus. Just let it rip. Put your heart into it and don't stop until the song is finished. You will notice that the atmosphere will change. A spirit of faith will rise. A power will be released that only comes through praise.

Power in Praise

The Bible has a lot to say about the power of praise. Psalm 22 says that God is "enthroned" on the praises of his people (vs. 3). If you want the power of God in your situation, start praising. In 2 Chronicles 20, the king's army routed the enemy, not with military force, but with songs of praise (vs. 22). And in Acts 16, Paul and Silas broke free from prison, not with human explosives, but with the power of praise (vs. 25-26).

David, perhaps more than any other character in the Bible, understood the power of praise. When the battle raged, David praised. And in the holy place of praise, God always spoke to him, comforted him, guided him and renewed him. One time, David found himself in the enemy territory of Gath when he was running from Saul. He was trying to find a safe place to escape Saul's murderous rampage, but the king of Gath was alerted to David's presence and turned against him. In this no-win situation (now David has two kings after his head!), David turned to praise.

According to its title, Psalm 34 was written during this episode in David's life. The opening lines of the psalm are, "I will bless the Lord at all times; his praise shall continually be in my mouth." How amazing is that? Even in David's place of utter desperation, the praises of God were still in his mouth. And not just sporadically, but *continually*. David woke up praising God and went to sleep praising God. He praised God when things went well, and even praised God for the setbacks. He could have easily complained. "Seriously, God? This is ridiculous! I'm trying to serve you and now all these kings want to kill me for no reason." Or doubted. "I thought you promised to protect me, God. I thought you promised me green pastures and quiet waters. I'm not sure this faith stuff even works!" Or blamed himself. "I always make stupid decisions and get myself into these situations. I know this is my fault, but what difference does it make now? I'm as good as dead."

But that's not what David did. Instead, he said, "Oh, taste and see that the LORD is good; Blessed is the man who trusts in Him!" (Psa 34:8 NKJV). David wasn't sinking back into an attitude of defeat and despair —he was boldly praising God and inviting others to join him. David was purposefully praising. And the atmosphere of praise filled David with faith. I'm sure he told his men, "Hey guys, don't get down. God is good! I know He will deliver us from this mess if we trust Him!" And, of course, that's exactly what happened. God gave David a unique solution and it worked. David feigned madness before the king of Gath, and the king let him go without any harm. God always has the last word, we just need to praise Him in the meantime!

You might not have two kings chasing you through the wilderness, but you are fighting with a loved one, or you received a bad report from the doctor, or your child is wandering far from God, or your boss is tormenting you. Don't wait for the situation to get better, start praising now. David didn't wait for the situation to resolve itself before he praised God. He woke up early on the day when everything was against him, went to his place of prayer and said, "I will bless the Lord at all times; his praise shall continually be in my mouth." Lesser men would have stayed in bed and cried. Not David. His attitude was, "Life is short, God is good, keep praising."

How I Learned to Praise

Praise is one of the greatest keys to living undefeated. Let praise be found in your mouth at all times. The Bible says to thank God in all things. Not some things, but all things. I remember when I first learned the power of praise in my own life. I had only been a Christian for a couple of years, and some friends invited me to a conference in the Pocono Mountains. It was at a quaint, rustic retreat center, and the topic that weekend was, "The Power of Praise." The speaker spoke so persuasively on praise that I purchased his book and read it that evening. The next day, during a break time, I ventured out into the woods behind the retreat center. I wanted to be alone and talk to God about an issue in my life. I didn't understand why God was taking so long to give me an answer.

"God, I'm going to praise you before I see the answer. Thank you for allowing me to go through these trials. You are worthy of my praise whether you give me what I ask for or not. I praise you, Lord. You know exactly what you're doing."

For the next couple of weeks, I woke up early and purposefully praised God. Whenever my thoughts drifted toward my unanswered prayer, I praised God. Throughout the day, I praised God. About one month later, God opened a door for me that I didn't know was there. He miraculously answered my prayer. And He did it in such a way that left me speechless. I remember saying to myself, "Wow, how did God just do that?" That was a turning point for me. To say that I became a big believer in praise is an understatement. The praises of God have become the soundtrack of my life, and I am convinced that much of my victory is the result of praise.

One of my Bible college professor used to say,

"If you only have ten minutes to pray, make nine of them praise."

How do you do that? Just thank God for who He is, all He does, and all He will do in your life. Don't complicate it. You already know how to praise—you do it all the time. When you eat at a really good restaurant, you praise it on Instagram. When you find a great show on Netflix, you tell all your friends about it. When your sports team wins, you tweet about how great they are. You already know how to praise. So just turn that praise towards God. Thank Him with your whole heart, and do it often. Wake up and purposefully praise Him. Praise him throughout the day. Praise Him when things go well and praise Him when things don't go well. In fact, be especially intentional about praising God when things don't go well. If you do, you will see a power released that will amaze you.

Enemies Routed by Praise

King Jehoshaphat had just received news that Judah was surrounded by enemy armies, and he was scared (2 Chron. 20). But he was about to learn the greatest lesson of his life on the power of praise. He immediately called the entire nation to fast and pray. They all gathered for a prayer and worship service, and in that service, a prophet stood up and gave a message to the people. It wasn't the message you might expect. He didn't say, "Be brave, oh Judah, God will be with you in war." He didn't say, "You will suffer many casualties, but in the end you will triumph." What he did say was,

"You will not need to fight in this battle" (2 Chr. 20:17).

Huh? They must have said, "We will not need to fight? There are three vicious armies marching against us right now, intent on destroying us!" But God's kingdom operates on different rules. In God's kingdom, prayer is more powerful than swords and praise is more powerful than spears. The prophet explained his message, "The battle is not yours but God's.... You will not need to fight in this battle. Stand firm, hold your position, and see the salvation of the Lord on your behalf, O Judah and Jerusalem" (2 Chron. 20:15-17). It was a radical message. The prophet was promising that God would literally fight for them. All they had to do was stand in faith and let God work. Perhaps God is telling you the same thing right now. Your battle may seem unwinnable, but God is telling you, "The battle is not yours, but mine. Let me fight it. Just stand in faith and praise me."

The next morning, the army of Judah went out to the battlefield, not to fight, but to stand. In front of the army, King Jehoshaphat sent the worship team to sing praises to God. Anyone watching this scene must have thought, "How ridiculous! This is a war. What kind of king would send out unarmed singers before his army to sing worship songs? Is this some kind of joke?" But I wonder what that observer would have said ten minutes later when this happened: "And when they began to sing and praise, the Lord set an ambush against the men of Ammon, Moab, and Mount Seir, who had come against Judah, so that they were routed" (2 Chr. 20:22). Routed. In other words, completely defeated, demolished, demoralized, destroyed. God did a supernatural work and made the enemy armies completely destroy one another. The Israelites didn't have to do a thing, except go in and collect the spoil. The next time the devil tells you praise is not powerful, read this passage to him.

There is power in praise! If God is telling you to stand instead of fight, trust him. Begin to praise and thank God daily. Your battle will not be won by human power. Something greater is required. God's divine power is what's needed, and that power is released by your praise.

"Because your love is better than life, my lips will glorify you. I will praise you as long as I live, and in your name I will lift up my hands" (Psa. 63:3-4).

Discussion Questions

1. Describe the current place that praise has in your life. Do you listen to worship music and/or sing to the Lord?
2. Share one story when praise and worship was particularly powerful or meaningful to you.
3. Which one of the Biblical stories about praise in this chapter impacted you the most, and why?
4. Do you find it more difficult to praise God when times are tough? How can you break through this mental obstacle to praise?
5. What are some practical ways that you can begin incorporating more praise into your life?

6

GOD FIRST

"When we put God first, all other things fall into their proper place or drop out of our lives."—Ezra T. Benson

YOU CAN ONLY LIVE the undefeated life if God is *first* in your life. God can't be third or second or even 'first and a half.' God must be supreme. When He is, everything else falls into place.

"But that's crazy," Karl said.

"I know," I said. "But that is what God is leading me to do." It was 1996 and I was a crossroads in my life. I had to decide who was first in my life. I was telling my friend Karl, who was never one to mince words, that God was leading me to leave New Jersey and move to Mexico. I had wrestled with the decision for some time, and had just recently progressed from "possibly, maybe, I think so," to "OK, I'm going to obey God, come hell or high water. Let's do this." Karl thought it was crazy that I was leaving the security of my life in America for an unknown future in a foreign country. "What about your career?" he asked. "It doesn't make sense that you went to college and earned a degree, and now you are going to skip off to a faraway land to do missionary work or something."

"I agree that it doesn't make sense, humanly speaking," I said. "But I've got time for a career later. I don't want to come to the end of my life and realize that I've missed God."

God had to be first. It wasn't that the other things didn't matter. Pursuing a career, starting a family, saving money for my first house—all of those things were important to me. But only one thing was *first*. It had to be God first and everything else second. I was determined to obey God, even if it meant delaying those other good things in my life. The amazing thing is that God eventually provided all those other things in ways I never dreamed of. My life is a testament to the truth, "If you put God first, you will never be last."

The undefeated life is the God-first life. When you put God first, it may be costly in the short-term, but it leads to a life of victory and prosperity over the long-term. I have never once regretted obeying God and moving to Mexico when I was twenty-six. I learned invaluable lessons there. I grew, I traveled, I matured. And best of all, I met the one person who has meant more to me than anyone else on the planet for the past twenty years, my beautiful wife Raquel! My life is richer and better in every way because I made the decision to put God first.

Evaluate Yourself

God has always required that His people put Him first. Some things are negotiable—this one is not. God's principle is: Put me first, and everything else in your life will prosper. When He gave His law to Moses, God wasn't shy about clarifying who was to be first. He didn't want to leave anything open to guesswork or interpretation. The first of the Ten Commandments emphatically states, "You shall have no other gods before me" (Deut. 5:7). That means there can be nothing before God, ahead of God, in place of God or competing with God. He must hold the undisputed top spot in your life.

How do you know if God is first in your life? Take some time and do an honest self-evaluation. Ask yourself if God is first in these areas of your life:

- **Finances.** Do I recognize that all of my money belongs to God? Am I faithful to dedicate the first 10% of everything that I earn to God?
- **Family.** Do my actions prove that my family comes before my career, my hobbies and my other pursuits?
- **Decisions.** Do I seek God's will first in my decision-making, or do I tack a quick prayer onto the end of my self-centered decision-making?
- **Time.** Is my time truly dedicated to God, even though it makes me uncomfortable or inconvenienced?
- **Priorities.** Would those around me say that my number one priority is God and His will?

IF YOU ARE wobbly on your answers to any of these questions, then perhaps you have some work to do. You might want to look at rearranging your priorities so that God truly occupies first place in your life. Here is the simple truth: today you will decide who or what is first in your life. Your actions will prove it. And tomorrow, you will decide again. And the next day, you will decide again. No one can make this decision for you—you must do it every day of your life.

Is it Worth It?

I admit that it's not easy putting God first in your life. The God-first life is not an easy, cushy, lazy life. It will require sacrifice from you. You will not always understand the way God is leading or agree with the way He does things. In the end, He is always proven right, but you only see that after you've come through the trial. So why should you go through the trouble of putting God first in your life? If it requires sacrifice and delayed gratification and difficulty, the question is, "Is it worth it?" Let me answer that question in four parts.

ONE: God is worth it. If God really is the Supreme Being in the universe, then all that I could possibly give Him is just a tiny fraction of what He is truly worth. He is worthy of all my devotion and much, much more. So instead of asking, "Is putting God first worth it to me?" ask, "Isn't God worth my absolute, unqualified best?"

One time, Raquel and I spent the night at the famous Waldorf Astoria hotel in New York City. We were awed by the opulence. They even gave us 'his' and 'her' bathrobes. A knock came on the door, and a man introduced himself as our Personal Valet. I couldn't think of anything for him to do for us (crazy, I know!), but I did have one question for him.

"What is the most expensive suite in this hotel?" I asked.

"That would be the Presidential Suite, sir," he replied.

"How much does it cost to stay there?" I asked.

"Up to $10,000 per night," he said. When he saw the surprised look on my face, he followed up with, "Isn't the President worth it, sir?"

If the leader of the free world is worth a pricey hotel suite, isn't the Leader of the universe worth our praise and devotion?

TWO: Idols promise much and deliver little. Idols always seem attractive at first. Money seems like a great provider, at first. False gods seem powerful and interesting, for a season. Wrong roads can be thrilling, for awhile. But idols always fail. They never deliver what they promise, because they are not able to. Only God can do God things. Idols are false and fallible by their very nature.

Former child actor Kirk Cameron found out that idols promise much more than they deliver. At age fourteen, he was one of the stars of the hit show, *Growing Pains*. "I had as much money as I wanted to spend. I was traveling around the world meeting famous people. I was a famous person. I had everything that I wanted," he said. But there was something missing in his life, and he knew it. When the father of the girl he liked invited him to church, he decided to give it a try. After hearing the sermon, Kirk felt guilty for his sins, yet full of hope in a loving God who would forgive and redeem him of his sins. He later dedicated his life to Christ and left Hollywood to become an evangelist. "I can honestly tell you today," he said, "that of all the places I've ever been, of all the people I've ever met, of all the fun and exciting things I've ever done, absolutely nothing compares to the joy of knowing Jesus Christ, of knowing that my sins are forgiven and that I'm in a right relationship with God."[1]

THREE: Where else would you go? If you decide to leave the one Source of goodness and light and love, where would you go? If God were not first in your life, what would you replace him with? All the other choices are paltry, puny and pitiful in comparison to the Creator and Sustainer of the universe.

When times are tough, you will be tempted to leave God. Peter faced this choice when many others were leaving Jesus. They loved Jesus when He gave them free bread and fish, but they tired of Him when He told them about the narrow and difficult way that leads to life. So they started leaving. As Jesus and the twelve stood and watched another group leaving, Jesus turned to His disciples and asked, "Do you want to go away as well?" (John 6:67). Peter's answer is heartfelt and powerful, and it's something I have said many times to the Lord, "Lord, to whom shall we go? You have the words of eternal life" (John 6:68). How can you go from the greater to the lesser? Once you have found Christ, you have reached the pinnacle. You've reached number one, and there is nowhere else to go.

FOUR: Blessing follows obedience. Is it worth it to put God first?

Only if you want to be chased down and overtaken by blessings! "And all these blessings shall come upon you and overtake you, if you obey the voice of the Lord your God" (Deut. 28:2). I don't know about you, but I want to be overtaken by blessings! Put God first and His blessings will overtake you. It's the promise of God. There have been countless times in my own life that God has proven this true to me. When Raquel and I rented our first house, God gave us twice the house that we could afford, in a neighborhood we couldn't afford, at less than half the price it should have cost. When we purchased our first home in New Jersey, once again God gave us much more house than we could afford in a neighborhood that was perfect for raising our children. When you put God first, you will never be last!

Giving up my Idols

"I'm ok, but the car had to be towed." I was standing on the side of the road talking on my cell phone in the cold, telling my wife what had happened. It's not the call I expected to make when I left the house to go for a quick run on the local trail. I was in a hurry, the roads were slick, and I collided with another car on a curve that was sharper than it looked.

That night, I sat alone talking to God about my predicament. "Lord, I really don't need this right now. I can't afford to fix my car or pay insurance surcharges. I need your help, Lord. I'm asking you to speak to me through your Word." I picked up my Bible and felt impressed to turn to Matthew 6. The thirty-third verse jumped out at me.

"But seek first the kingdom of God and his righteousness, and all these things will be added to you."

"Lord, you know I try, with all my heart, to seek you first in my life. I want your will to be done, not mine. Is there any area of my life where you are not first? If so, please tell me, and I will deal with it," I said. Immediately, I felt that the Holy Spirit spoke to me, "Your marathon running is an idol."

"Wait a minute, Lord," I said. "There is no way that my running is an idol. It keeps me healthy! I admit that it takes a lot of my time and attention, but I have it under control. You're not asking me to give up running, are you?" I didn't hear an answer from the Lord. But I knew He was dealing with an area of my life that I did not want Him to touch. The fact is, I loved running. A lot. It had been my outlet, my therapy, my hobby and my passion for more than a decade. It had become a large part of my identity. The thought of giving up running was, frankly, horrifying. It hurts when God puts His hand on your idol.

I was convinced that I could live the God-first life and still be a passionate runner, but I had to admit that during this season of my life, running had become like a part-time job. I was training for a marathon, and that meant everything else took second place. My training came first. My weekend plans were formed around my running. I regularly sacrificed time with my family because my running program called for a one-hour run. Even my morning prayer time was cut short because of the demands of my training. Could it be true that running had become an idol in my life?

I wasn't ready to admit that yet. But I couldn't stop thinking about what God had told me. I wrestled with it, I went back and forth, until finally, three weeks later, I came to the point of full surrender. "OK God," I said. "If you want me to give up running, I will. I don't want anything, even a good thing like running, to come between you and me." A sense of great peace came over me. I knew God was using this to draw me closer to Himself.

The next month or so was cathartic. I canceled my marathon plans and ramped up my prayer and devotional life again. It felt wonderful, liberating, refreshing. My life moved back into balance again. Sure, I missed running, but I needed this time to reorient my priorities. I eventually returned to running, and I still run to this day, but I hold it very loosely now. Running is a great blessing in my life, but it will never rule me again. It will never compete with the One who is first.

Letting Go

Letting go of your idols is not easy. We are experts at rationalizing our choices and have the perverse desire to protect our idols at any cost. Why do we do that? We have a generous and loving Father who wants to give us much more than He takes away. He is not trying to rob you of joy—He is trying to remove everything that impedes His joy, the only true joy, from flowing in your life. If the Giver of true joy puts His hand on an idol in your life, let Him take it away! He doesn't need to be first place in your life—you need Him to be in first place. You lose if God is not first, and God knows that. As a wise and loving Father, He wants to bring you to that place where you willingly lay down your idols and let the Giver of true joy occupy the number one spot in your life.

Be honest right now. Ask yourself this question, "Is there anything in my life that competes with God for my time and attention? Do I often wake up in the morning thinking about something else, instead of God first? When I am stressed, do I often run to something else, instead of God?" If you answered 'yes' to any of these questions, then you probably have an idol in your life. I urge you to deal with it and find the true freedom that comes from laying down everything that competes with God, and enthroning Him alone as the undisputed king of your life.

One Thing You Lack

There are times in our lives when we have several things right but one thing wrong, and that one thing wrong is really wrong. Instead of correcting the thing we have wrong, our tendency is to boast about the things we have right, while ignoring the wrong. A rich young ruler found himself in this exact situation one day when he ran into Jesus. He engaged Jesus in conversation as the disciples listened. The young man was cocky. He asked Jesus a question, and he thought he already knew the answer.

"Good Teacher, what must I do to inherit eternal life?" (Luke 18:18).

He wasn't looking for information—he was looking to make a point. He wanted to prove to everyone watching that he knew the way to eternal life. He was sure that he had kept all of God's commandments, so he figured this was going to be a slam dunk. Jesus, however, knew that you don't get into heaven by following commandments—you get into heaven by following a Person. Jesus put His finger on the one thing that was standing between the young ruler and eternal life. It was his idol. The young ruler didn't think he had an idol. But Jesus knew that he did. And Jesus loved him enough to confront him and challenge him to lay it down.

> "One thing you still lack. Sell all that you have and distribute to the poor, and you will have treasure in heaven; and come, follow me" (Luke 18:22).

Jesus challenged him to lay down his idol of money. That was the one thing he lacked: freedom from the love of money. This young ruler wanted to boast about all the good things he had done, but Jesus would not let him off the hook. "That's great," Jesus was saying, "but you *must* deal with this one thing, because if you don't, it will keep you from me. Your unhealthy obsession with money will make you miss heaven." The young ruler thought about it for a second, then shook his head and walked away sad. It was inconceivable to him that he should give up any of his possessions. In that one moment of time, he chose to cling to death and allow life to slip through his fingers. God's Son was standing right in front of him, offering him eternal joy and peace and happiness forever and ever, and he said, "Nah, I'll stick with my stuff here on earth." How tragic.

When we read this story, it seems crazy to us that anyone would give up eternal life and walk away from the Son of God. For what? Stuff? Possessions? Fame? Sex? Power? But we do the same thing, don't we? Anytime we allow an idol to exist and persist in our lives, we are walking away from the Son of God.

Hundredfold Blessings

The good news is, the story doesn't end there. Peter and the other apostles were listening to this interchange between Jesus and the young ruler, and Peter now had a question for Jesus. "See, we have left everything and followed you. What then will we have?" (Matt. 19:27). Peter is saying, "Lord, I left my fishing business to follow you. All of us have made significant sacrifices to put you first in our lives. Is it all worth it, Lord? What will we receive?" Jesus had a clear and succinct answer. "What will you receive, Peter? You will receive a hundredfold." A hundredfold. In other words, you will receive back one hundred times what you put in. Whatever you sacrifice for God will seem paltry in comparison with what you receive back. You can't outgive God. "Everyone who has left houses or brothers or sisters or father or mother or children or lands, for my name's sake, will receive a hundredfold and will inherit eternal life" (Matt. 19:29). When you put God first, you will be blessed one hundredfold. You may have to make sacrifices, but you will receive one hundredfold blessings in return, *plus* you will inherit eternal life. I think that's a really good deal!

Peter was blessed one hundredfold. He started out as a nondescript fisherman on a lonely Galilean lake and ended up as the first megachurch pastor, with thousands of people under his care. Jenn, a friend of mine, gave up a six-figure job in banking to serve as a children's pastor in a small church. She did such an outstanding job that she was eventually hired by a large, multi-site church and now oversees ten campus children's pastors. God takes the humble and obscure and places them in high positions when they choose to put Him first.

WHAT ABOUT YOU? Are you putting God first? If you are, let me encourage you: God sees your sacrifice. God sees that you could have gotten a better job, but you cared about your family time, so you accepted the lower position. God sees that you could have gotten the prettier girl or the cuter guy, but you wanted to be with a true Christian, so you chose inner character over outward perfection. God sees that you could have had more fame and notoriety, but you chose to humbly serve behind the scenes and make Jesus famous. God sees and God rewards you one hundredfold. If you have put God first and don't see your hundredfold blessing yet, keep going. Don't grow weary, your harvest is coming. It may be delayed for a season, but God is never late. If you put God first, you will never be last.

Discussion Questions

1. If you had to identify the one area of your life that has the most potential to compete with God for your time and attention, what would you say it is?
2. We know to reject evil, but how do things that are good become idols in our lives and rob us of God's best?
3. Read Matthew 6:33 and share how you can live out this verse in your life.
4. Discuss the benefits of putting God first in your life.
5. How would your life look different if God were truly first-place in your time, in your finances, in your family, in your plans?
6. What is one change you can make to place God first in your life, starting this week?

7
IT NEVER GETS OLD

"Believers are strong only as the Word of God abides in them. The Word of God is spirit and life to those who receive it in simple faith . . . Know your Book, live it, believe it, and obey it. Hide God's word in your heart. It will save your soul, quicken your body, illumine your mind. The Word of God is full and final, infallible, reliable, and up-to-date, and our attitude towards it must be one of unquestioned obedience."—Smith Wigglesworth

"WHAT AN IDIOT," I thought. I was around twenty-one years old, and I was driving to a midweek church service. The object of my wrath was the driver of an old, brown Ford who pulled out in front of me and proceeded at a snail's pace. "Is this guy serious?" I said. "I'm going to be late!" I walked into church flustered and angry. In the foyer, I encountered my friend Tom and he must have noticed the look on my face.

"What happened, did somebody cut you off?" he asked.

"Ha, yeah," I replied. I was thinking, "Sheesh, how did Tom know? Am I really known for my temper?" A quick temper. It's what I grew up with. It's what I knew, as a New Jersey native of Irish descent. I had learned to react to life rather passionately. Then, at nineteen, I became a follower of Christ and everything changed. My habits, my desires, my circle of friends—everything became brand new. Except for one thing. After a couple of years as a Christian, I noticed there was one area of my old life that still clung to me: my thought life. On a good day, my thoughts were good. On a bad day, my thoughts were ugly, carnal and messy. "I don't like my anger anymore," I confessed to Tom after church. "But I can't seem to get it under control."

"I totally get it," he said. "I used to be the same way. I was known as the 'mean one.' I tried to get better but never succeeded. Then I discovered the power of the Word."

"What do you mean?" I asked.

"The Bible is powerful," he said. "It's a special book. It never gets old, and it never loses its power. I found that when I upgrade my thoughts to God's thoughts, I succeed. When my thoughts rise up and get the better of me, I fail. I recommend that you upgrade your angry thoughts to God's thoughts."

I had been reading the Bible every day, and I loved how full of faith it made me feel. But I wasn't intentionally upgrading my negative thoughts to God's thoughts from the Bible.

"That's a great idea. Thanks Tom!" I said.

Embedding the Word

The first thing I did when I got home was pull out the Book that never gets old and never loses its power. I looked up all the verses that dealt with anger. I found almost thirty of them. I figured that if I had any hope of replacing my toxic thinking with God's pure Word, I needed every one of these verses embedded into my heart. So I wrote them all down on one sheet of paper and read through that list every morning. My favorite passage was James 1:19-20, "My dear brothers and sisters, take note of this: Everyone should be quick to listen, slow to speak and slow to become angry, because human anger does not produce the righteousness that God desires." Every time I would get mad, I would repeat this Scripture to myself. It had no effect at first. In fact, it just made me angrier! "Why are you bringing the Bible into this?" I would say to myself. "Because you need it!" I would answer back.

If You Can Make It There

With time, God's words began to have a noticeable effect in my life. His thoughts began to replace my thoughts. It was amazing. The first time I noticed a real change was the day I drove into New York City. It should come as no surprise that driving in New York City can spark fits of anger, even among the meek and mild-mannered. But my reactions were different that day. Someone cut me off and I said, "Bless you in Jesus' name." Someone else almost hit me and I said, "Thank you, Father, for that man. Bless his life right now." A huge bus almost squeezed me against the side of the Lincoln Tunnel and I said, "Thank you for this day, Lord. I trust you for my safety." What was happening to me? No fits of anger? No one-finger waves out the window? No ten-second horn salutes? This Bible stuff was really working!

God's Word was changing me. I was no longer the angry man I once was. God's thoughts had penetrated my mind and replaced my toxic thoughts with His thoughts of life and peace. It was one of the most beautiful things I've ever experienced. And I'm happy to say that it's been twenty-five years since that day in New York City, and I've never gone back to the old, angry Dave I used to be.

There are times when we search for the answer to something, but the solution is right in front of us. Don't look any further than your Bible if you want freedom and power. You may be struggling with wrong thinking, depression, fear or anxiety. The Word has the power to meet the greatest challenges in your life.

How to Have Good Success

I mentioned in Chapter Four that one of my favorite verses in the Bible is Joshua 1:8,

"This Book of the Law shall not depart from your mouth, but you shall meditate on it day and night, so that you may be careful to do according to all that is written in it. For then you will make your way prosperous, and then you will have good success."

God is telling us how to have good success! Let's take a moment and look more closely at this verse.

The context is that God is preparing Joshua to lead one million Israelites across the Jordan River to fight for the land He has promised them. It's a huge and complex task, and the potential for failure is high. In this one verse, God tells Joshua exactly what he needs to do in order to guarantee victory.

"This Book of the Law." Joshua has his own copy of the Bible, which at that time only contained the Law of Moses. Joshua doesn't have to rely on hearsay or the opinions of men. He has the written Word of God. He is able to consult the Scriptures every morning and find answers for every question, every difficulty and every challenge. Can I make a recommendation for your life? Buy a leather Bible. Make it a good one. Turn it into your best friend and consult it every morning. The Bible will never let you down. In today's world of digital Bibles, I still believe in old-fashioned leather Bibles. There is something precious about the printed Scriptures that will move you, inspire you and guide you. Go ahead and underline verses and make notes in your Bible. They say a Bible that's falling apart usually belongs to someone who isn't.

"Shall not depart from your mouth." How interesting that the first thing God wants Joshua to do with his Word is to speak it. There is power in the tongue. You only confess what you really believe. God is saying, "If you really believe what I'm saying, Joshua, tell other people about it! Speak my Word. Share it openly. Declare the promises out loud. Never be ashamed to confess my Word in front of men." How often do we read the Scripture or hear a sermon and let it die? We close our mouths because we are afraid or ashamed to openly confess God's Word before men, and therefore the Scripture never bears fruit in our

lives. God says that the next step after hearing God's Word is to speak it, and never let it depart from our mouth.

"Meditate on it day and night." Joshua is a busy man, but God commands him to take time "day and night" and meditate on His Word. I estimate that this would take no less than one hour per day. If God required the commander-in-chief of a large, wartime army to spend one hour per day thinking on and speaking Scripture, how much time should you spend daily? Perhaps a bit more time than you are spending now? Meditating on God's Word is not a casual endeavor. It takes focus, effort and intentionality. I recommend a simple system like the SOAP method (Scripture, Observation, Application, Prayer), in which you read one chapter of the Bible per day and record in a journal your observations, personal life applications and prayer. You will be amazed at the power of this simple system.[1]

"So that you might be careful to do according to all that is written in it." God does not want Joshua to come to his Word for information only— He expects Joshua to actually obey what is written. Never come to the Bible as a hearer only. Come to the Bible determined to do everything it says. God is not interested in puffing up your mind with knowledge. God wants to change your life. Every time you open the Bible, pray this prayer, "God, I come to your Word hungry to receive life. I will believe what you tell me and obey what you command me. Replace my thoughts with your thoughts and give me victory today. In Jesus' name, amen."

"For then you will make your way prosperous, and then you will have good success." This is the promise. God promises prosperity and good success to those who replace their thoughts with His thoughts and obey what His Word says. What a phenomenal pledge! I urge you to take this promise at face value and believe it. Don't say, "Be careful now. Don't promise people too much." That would be a fair warning if I invented this promise myself. But it's not my promise—it's God's promise! Have all the emotions you want. God has gone on record and unequivocally says, "If you believe my Word, meditate on my Word, speak my Word and obey my Word, I promise that you will have good

success." Joshua held tightly to God's Word, and he enjoyed decades of good success in the Promised Land.

Objections to the Word

When I say that the power is in the Word and encourage you to memorize the Word and speak the Word, you may notice a reaction in your heart. You might have some resistance to the idea of relying so heavily on the Bible. Because I know how the enemy relentlessly attacks God's Word, let me address a couple of concerns I've heard.

1. **The Bible was written by men.** The truth is, the Bible was written by men, but inspired by God. Paul says, "All Scripture is breathed out [or, inspired] by God" (2 Tim. 3:16). Men wrote down the words, but they are God's words. Moses received the Law directly from God; the prophets wrote down the exact messages God gave them; the Gospel writers wrote down Jesus' exact words.
2. **The Bible was written for that time only.** There are portions of the Bible that are historical narrative or descriptive of a certain time and place, but the Bible's teachings are timeless. It's always wrong, in all times and places, to cheat on your wife. It's always right, in every culture, to do good unto your neighbor.
3. **The Bible has contradictions in it.** No, actually, the Bible is a marvel of unity in its teachings. The supposed contradictions have all been answered convincingly. It's astounding how sixty-six books can blend together so seamlessly, all of them pointing to one God and his only Son Jesus Christ.
4. **I don't understand the Bible.** The Holy Spirit was sent to "guide you into all the truth" (John 16:13). If you ask Him, the Holy Spirit will help you understand the Bible. I know someone who was illiterate as an adult when he came to

Christ. He desperately wanted to read the Bible, so one day, he picked up a Bible and asked God to help him understand the words. God did a miracle, and he understood what he was reading. He read the entire Bible and afterward started to read other books. He went on to earn his high school degree and multiple college degrees. If you ever open the Bible and say, "I don't understand this," can I make you a promise? If you come to the Word with the right attitude, God will always help you understand His Word. Don't shy away from the Word because it's difficult—persevere through the difficulty and reap the rich rewards. The truth is, much of the Bible is eminently understandable. "Love God . . . love your neighbor . . . seek first God's kingdom . . . walk by faith not by sight." These are not difficult things to understand. What's difficult, of course, is the obeying part. As Mark Twain said, "It ain't those parts of the Bible that I can't understand that bother me, it is the parts that I do understand." Twain was admitting that God's Word is clear and compelling—it's the obeying part that bothered him!

Only the Hungry are Fed

One of the most powerful concepts I have learned (and have had to re-learn many times) is that in the kingdom, only the hungry are fed. Jesus will feed you His richest truths, but only if you are hungry for them. I saw this illustrated once when I was in the Dominican Republic on a missions trip. We were ministering in a care center that specialized in feeding and tutoring underprivileged children. I asked the director how she kept up with the overwhelming needs of the impoverished area in which she ministered.

"The children have to play by our rules," she said. "If they don't attend our religious services, they don't eat. If they mistreat one another, they don't eat. If they don't bring their homework, they don't eat. By doing this, we ensure that only the hungry are fed."

I think the same thing applies to understanding the Bible: only the hungry are fed. If you come to Bible flippantly, casually and hurriedly, you will not be fed. If, however, you come to the Bible as a beggar desperate to unlock its sacred storehouse of treasure, you will be fed abundantly. It will cost you a bit of time and effort. But if you persevere, the Word of God will feed your soul in a way that nothing else can.

Don't Lose Your Hunger

One of the curses of modern-day America is that we are overfed. We have such an abundance of everything, yet we appreciate nothing. There are over 47,000 items on the shelves of the average American grocery store. Many of us suffer from some degree of *affluenza*, the "unhealthy and unwelcome psychological and social effects of affluence."[2] You may not feel rich, but compared to previous generations and to the majority of people alive today outside the United States, you are well-off. This affluence has one devastating effect: it blunts your hunger. As a general rule, American Christians are not known for their hungry, passionate, pay-any-price, willing-to-die-for-the-faith attitude toward Christianity. Many of us have lost our hunger.

When you lose your hunger for the Word of God, everything else begins to decay. Your faith, your love, your obedience, your witness, your service to others and your worship all decline if the Word of God loses its luster in your eyes. Let me humbly warn you: Never lose your hunger for the Word of God! If you feel your hunger waning, stop everything and cry out to God to give you a fresh hunger. Don't continue going through the motions–the fumes that you are running on will eventually run out. Get intentional about this. We are talking about the health of your own soul. Take an entire day and go to a secluded place with just your Bible and a notebook. Ask God to speak to you, and He will. Ask Him to renew a love for the Bible in your heart, and He will. Ask Him to give you that old fire again, and He will.

The Word Never Returns Void

God makes many promises about the power of His Word, but one of the most precious is found in Isaiah 55:10-11,

> For as the rain and the snow come down from heaven
> and do not return there but water the earth,
> making it bring forth and sprout,
> giving seed to the sower and bread to the eater,
> so shall my word be that goes out from my mouth;
> it shall not return to me empty,
> but it shall accomplish that which I purpose,
> and shall succeed in the thing for which I sent it.

God promises that His Word shall not return empty, or void. When He sends forth His Word, it *will* accomplish that which He purposes. Awesome! We are used to things coming back void: failed efforts, frustrated dreams, botched plans. But not God. When He purposes something, it is done. When He predicts something, it happens. When He speaks something, it is fulfilled. Let this be good news to you today: the promises God has made for your life *will* be fulfilled. It may take longer than you want and happen in a way you don't expect, but God will fulfill His promises to you.

Shouldn't you stop worrying and obsessing and complaining and doubting? Wouldn't it be a better use of your time to remind yourself daily of God's promises and thank Him for fulfilling them in your life?

Use the Word

My old friend Ron is an example of a man who knows that God's Word does not return void. Ron is one of the most positive, faith-filled, encouraging people I've ever met. The first time I visited his home, I was struck by the fact that he had hung a bulletin board in the front hallway, on the way to the kitchen. On it were tacked cards with handwritten Scripture verses.

"What's this?" I asked.

"That's my Scripture wall," he said. "Every morning, when I come downstairs for my coffee, I read through these verses out loud." I read some of the verses he had posted.

> "No weapon that is formed against you will prosper" (Isaiah 54:17 NASB).
> "The Lord will accomplish what concerns me" (Psalm 138:8 NASB).
> "The Lord is my shepherd, I shall not want" (Psalm 23:1 NASB).

"That's pretty cool," I said. "So you read all these verses out loud every morning?"

"I do. I learned a long time ago that God's Word never returns void," he said. "I start my day by declaring His powerful Word and leaving the rest to him."

"I love it," I said. "But why do you think so few Christians wake up with the Word like you do?"

"Because they haven't been taught to *use* the Word," he said. "The Word is just a book on the shelf to them. It doesn't do us much good on a shelf, does it? We need to take the promises, personalize them and *use* them. God's Word is just as powerful today as when God said, 'Let there be,' and the universe was created."

"That's true, Ron," I said, "So has the Word made a difference in your life?"

"It's made all the difference," Ron said. "I used to go to church and learn the Word, but I wasn't *using* the Word. And then my wife and I struggled through a season where she couldn't get pregnant. That really drove me to the promises. I began to do more than just read the Word, I began to stand on the Word. I started to actually believe the Word. I said, 'God, you call those things that are not as though they are, so I am believing you and thanking you now for the child you will give us, before it comes to pass.' And we eventually did get that child. It took us two long years to get pregnant, but God gave us a healthy baby girl!"

"So standing on the promises really works," I said.

"Oh, it works better than you think," Ron answered. "After having our first daughter, we went on to have five more children. His Word never returns void!"

Discussion Questions

1. Describe your current interaction with God's Word. Are you reading the Bible daily?
2. Describe a time when you stood on a promise of God and it came to pass for you.
3. What does God say we must do in order to have "good success" in Joshua 1:8? Are you practicing this verse in your life?
4. What objections have you had about the Word of God (name doubts or concerns you have had about the Bible)?
5. What is one area of your life in which you will start confessing the powerful Word of God?

8
THE NEW YOU

"Your identity is not in your sin. Your identity is in your Savior."—Mark Driscoll

WHO YOU ARE today is not who you used to be. Knowing who you are in Christ is absolutely essential to walking in victory. If you want to live the undefeated life, learn who the Bible says you are in Christ and walk in that new identity. In Christ, you are redeemed, you are chosen, you are free. Your old life is dead and you have a new purpose and a new calling. That's your new identity! But be warned, even though you are brand-new in Christ, the devil will try to convince you that you are not new at all. He specializes in reminding you of your old life and pulling you back to your old identity, the person you were before making Jesus the Lord of your life. You must resist this and reassert your new identity every single day.

After I became a follower of Christ and left my old life behind, I sat down with Adam, one of my old friends from college. "Do you remember that time you were so wasted that you almost punched the police horse in the mouth?" Adam asked. I just smiled and waited for him to stop laughing. Adam saw that I wasn't laughing, but charged ahead anyway and regaled me with stories of my old life before Christ at Rutgers University. Some of the stories were comical, sure, but I hadn't called Adam to have lunch so we could rehash stories about my old life. I wanted to tell him about my new life in Christ.

"You know what?" I finally said. "That old Dave is dead." Adam looked at me like I was smoking some of that herb.

"But I'm looking right at him," Adam said.

"No, actually, the Dave you are looking at now is a a different Dave," I said. "Jesus has made me a new man and my past is completely dead. All things have become new for me." I proceeded to tell Adam about the amazing changes in my life since becoming a new creature in Christ.

"Good for you, Dave," he said. "But I don't think you should deny who you once were."

"I fully accept who I once was, Adam. I was lost and sinful and stupid. But at the same time, I can't deny who I have become. I am a new person in Christ. I am redeemed and forgiven and renewed. God has truly changed me and given me purpose in life!"

Something Dramatic Happened

When you came to Christ, something dramatic happened. Your conversion experience may have been calm and quiet or profound and earth-shattering. That doesn't matter. What matters is that God placed you in Christ the moment you gave your heart to Jesus. You might have felt nothing, or you might have seen the heavens opened and heard angels singing. Again, that's inconsequential. What matters is that you were given a new identity in that instant. Whether you whispered a quiet prayer in your living room, or bellowed, "I believe!" through tears at a revival service, your old identity died in that moment and you became a new creature in Christ.

"Therefore, if anyone is in Christ, he is a new creation. The old has passed away; behold, the new has come" (2 Cor. 5:17).

This is your verse! Go ahead and get a tattoo of this verse, memorize it, repeat it, rehearse it, never forget it. It establishes this one life-changing, revolutionary, mind-blowing truth: you are a brand-new creature in Christ. No one can ever take this away from you. In all your ups and downs, you are a new creation. Whatever life throws at you, you are a new creation. Even on your worst days, you are a new creation.

When I came to Christ, I experienced a noticeable conversion from darkness to light. I went from being drunk and stoned every day to being high on God. I went from being a lover of Jack Daniels, Jim Beam and Jameson to a lover of Matthew, Mark, Luke and John. All of my friends and family noticed the change in my lifestyle. You may not have had such a distinct experience when you came to Christ. Not everyone does. But if, at some point, you repented of your sins and believed on Jesus for salvation, you are just as brand-new as I am. You must believe that, insist on that and begin reinforcing it every day of your life. You are a new person in Christ. The old has passed away and no longer has any power over you. Don't look back—keep looking ahead, speaking ahead and moving ahead.

In Christ

The key to living in your new identity is realizing who you are *in Christ*. The word "Christian" occurs only three times in the Bible, while the terms "in Christ," "in the Lord," and "in Him" occur 164 times. If you want to live the undefeated life, remind yourself who you are in Christ every day.

Joyce Meyer has a fantastic list of Scripture verses on her website that tell you who you are in Christ.[1] I can't improve on this list, so I give it to you here in full. If you want to be reminded of your new identity in Christ, read this list of forty-six powerful truth out loud every day:

Who I Am in Christ

1. I am complete in Him Who is the head over all rule and authority—of every angelic and earthly power (Colossians 2:10).
2. I am alive with Christ (Ephesians 2:5).
3. I am free from the law of sin and death (Romans 8:2).
4. I am far from oppression, and will not live in fear (Isaiah 54:14).
5. I am born of God, and the evil one does not touch me (1 John 5:18).
6. I am holy and without blame before Him in love (Ephesians 1:4; 1 Peter 1:16).
7. I have the mind of Christ (1 Corinthians 2:16; Philippians 2:5).
8. I have the peace of God that surpasses all understanding (Philippians 4:7).
9. The Spirit of God, who is greater than the enemy in the world, lives in me (1 John 4:4).
10. I have received abundant grace and the gift of righteousness and reign in life through Jesus Christ (Romans 5:17).
11. I have received the Spirit of wisdom and revelation in the knowledge of Jesus, the eyes of my heart enlightened, so that I know the hope of having life in Christ (Ephesians 1:17-18).
12. I have received the power of the Holy Spirit and He can do miraculous things through me. I have authority and power over the enemy in this world (Mark 16:17-18; Luke 10:17-19).
13. I am renewed in the knowledge of God and no longer want to live in my old ways or nature before I accepted Christ (Colossians 3:9-10).
14. I am merciful, I do not judge others, and I forgive quickly. As I do this by God's grace, He blesses my life (Luke 6:36-38).
15. God supplies all of my needs according to His riches in glory in Christ Jesus (Philippians 4:19).

16. In all circumstances I live by faith in God and extinguish all the flaming darts (attacks) of the enemy (Ephesians 6:16).
17. I can do whatever I need to do in life through Christ Jesus who gives me strength (Philippians 4:13).
18. I am chosen by God who called me out of the darkness of sin and into the light and life of Christ so I can proclaim the excellence and greatness of who He is (1 Peter 2:9).
19. I am born again—spiritually transformed, renewed and set apart for God's purpose—through the living and everlasting word of God (1 Peter 1:23).
20. I am God's workmanship, created in Christ to do good works that He has prepared for me to do (Ephesians 2:10).
21. I am a new creation in Christ (2 Corinthians 5:17).
22. In Christ, I am dead to sin—my relationship to it is broken —and alive to God—living in unbroken fellowship with Him (Romans 6:11).
23. The light of God's truth has shone in my heart and given me knowledge of salvation through Christ (2 Corinthians 4:6).
24. As I hear God's Word, I do what it says and I am blessed in my actions (James 1:22, 25).
25. I am a joint-heir with Christ (Romans 8:17). I am more than a conqueror through Him who loves me (Romans 8:37).
26. I overcome the enemy of my soul by the blood of the Lamb and the word of my testimony (Revelation 12:11).
27. I have everything I need to live a godly life and am equipped to live in His divine nature (2 Peter 1:3-4).
28. I am an ambassador for Christ (2 Corinthians 5:20). I am part of a chosen generation, a royal priesthood, a holy nation, a purchased people (1 Peter 2:9).
29. I am the righteousness of God—I have right standing with Him—in Jesus Christ (2 Corinthians 5:21).
30. My body is a temple of the Holy Spirit; I belong to Him (1 Corinthians 6:19).

31. I am the head and not the tail, and I only go up and not down in life as I trust and obey God (Deuteronomy 28:13).
32. I am the light of the world (Matthew 5:14).
33. I am chosen by God, forgiven and justified through Christ. I have a compassionate heart, kindness, humility, meekness and patience (Romans 8:33; Colossians 3:12).
34. I am redeemed—forgiven of all my sins and made clean—through the blood of Christ (Ephesians 1:7).
35. I have been rescued from the domain and the power of darkness and brought into God's kingdom (Colossians 1:13).
36. I am redeemed from the curse of sin, sickness, and poverty (Deuteronomy 28:15-68; Galatians 3:13).
37. My life is rooted in my faith in Christ and I overflow with thanksgiving for all He has done for me (Colossians 2:7).
38. I am called to live a holy life by the grace of God and to declare His praise in the world (Psalm 66:8; 2 Timothy 1:9).
39. I am healed and whole in Jesus (Isaiah 53:5; 1 Peter 2:24).
40. I am saved by God's grace, raised up with Christ and seated with Him in heavenly places (Ephesians 2:5-6; Colossians 2:12).
41. I am greatly loved by God (John 3:16; Ephesians 2:4; Colossians 3:12; 1 Thessalonians 1:4).
42. I am strengthened with all power according to His glorious might (Colossians 1:11).
43. I humbly submit myself to God, and the devil flees from me because I resist him in the Name of Jesus (James 4:7).
44. I press on each day to fulfill God's plan for my life because I live to please Him (Philippians 3:14).
45. I am not ruled by fear because the Holy Spirit lives in me and gives me His power, love and self-control (2 Timothy 1:7).
46. Christ lives in me, and I live by faith in Him and His love for me (Galatians 2:20).

READING this list daily will renew your heart and transform your mind. Don't let the enemy steal these precious truths from you! You might say to me, "Am I just supposed to read this list of verses every morning and *voila* I'm a new person?" Well, first of all, kudos on using the word "voila," and second of all, you already are a new person in Christ. Reading this list merely reaffirms and reasserts who you already are in Him. The enemy constantly tries to drag you backward. This list of truths pushes you forward. Why do we need to be reminded so often? Because we are incredibly forgetful. Scientists say that we forget 50% of the information we learn after twenty minutes, and 75% after one day. We need constant reminders of who we are in Christ.

Talk Back to the Enemy

When the enemy or the flesh try to tell you that you haven't changed, you need to talk back! Many years ago, I was driving home after a particularly hard day. I was feeling beat up and frustrated. Just then, I drove by the liquor store that I used to frequent before becoming a new creature in Christ. "That's what you need," the enemy whispered to me. "A few beers will relax you and make everything better." I was at the stoplight and had a choice to either go straight or make a right turn into the liquor store parking lot. My hand was on the blinker.

"Maybe that is what I need," I thought. Before I could turn the car, however, something hit me. A holy anger rose up within me. I decided to talk back to the enemy. "Wait a minute. You're not gonna do that to me, devil! That's not who I am anymore! That's the old Dave, and he's dead. Old things have passed away and behold, all things have become new. I choose to get high on the joy of the Lord and to be filled with the Holy Spirit!" I hit the gas and went straight through that stoplight with a shout of victory. The person in the car next to me might have thought I was strange, but I didn't care. I had victory. I never went back to that liquor store, and I've never missed it.

When the enemy talks to you, talk back! When he tries to remind you of your old life, remind him of your new life. The devil is an expert at bringing up the old. Become an expert at bringing up the new.

Tune in to the New Channel

You've got to tune out the voices of the devil and the flesh, and tune in the voice of the Holy Spirit. The devil's radio channel tells you that you are a failure, that you are a sinner, that you are hopeless. That's the only channel you listened to for years. Because of this, you walked in sin and defeat. But when you came to Christ, something changed. A brand-new channel was added to your spectrum. This new channel tells you who you are in Christ, it reminds you of the promises of God, and it inspires you to believe God for greater things. Which channel are you listening to? If you are a Christian and all you listen to is the old channel, you will live in defeat. Why would you do that? Change the channel! Listen to what God says and fill yourself with the awesome truths of your new life and power and victory in Christ.[2]

Marlena started coming to my church about a year ago. She had recently come out of an abusive relationship and struggled greatly with her self-image. My wife met with her regularly and built her up on the promises of God and the truths of what it means to be a new creature in Christ. Several months ago, I saw her in the foyer after church, and asked her how she was doing. "Are you staying strong in the Word and rejecting the lies of the enemy?" I asked.

"I sure am!" she said, "My secret is Hillsong Worship. I listen to it every day and it keeps me strong in the Lord. My favorite song is, 'Who You Say I Am.'"

"Good choice!" I said. Thank God for the gift of music which enables us to not only glorify our Creator, but also to keep our spirits saturated with good and godly thoughts. The song "Who You Say I Am" contains these lyrics:

> I am chosen

Not forsaken
I am who You say I am
You are for me
Not against me
I am who You say I am[3]

That is something you should be reminded of daily!

Pick Up the Hammer

Your identity will have an outcome, because belief affects behavior. If you believe you are in chains, you will live your life as a prisoner. It's possible that everything in your life up until now has confirmed that you are a prisoner: your dad told you that you would never make it, your boss fired you, those closest to you don't believe in you. And besides this, your own mind tells you daily, "You are in chains!" The only way out of this bondage is pick up the hammer. You need to get a fire in your belly and smash this mindset once and for all. God said to Jeremiah, "Is not my word like fire, declares the Lord, and like a hammer that breaks the rock in pieces?" (Jer. 23:29). Pick up the Word of God like hammer and smash your old, toxic mindsets to pieces. Dr. Neil Anderson calls this a "truth encounter" in his books, *The Bondage Breaker* and *Victory Over Darkness*, which I highly recommend. He says,

> "We need to believe and confess what the Bible says about who we are in Christ. You don't 'out muscle' or 'out shout' the devil; you 'out truth' him. We need to say the Scriptures out loud! Yes, we need to believe, declare and act on the word of God; the devil is not obligated to obey our thoughts. When we truly assume the responsibility for our own life and believe the truth regardless of our sad emotions, we will find freedom."[4]

Take the hammer of God's Word and smash your old mindsets.

They have not produced anything good in your life. Break free! Declare right now,

> "Jesus Christ is my Lord and Savior. Old things have passed away and all things have become new. I am not a prisoner to my old sins and addictions. They are all broken, in Jesus' name. I receive the new anointing and new purpose and new blessing that God has for me today."

Healthy Beliefs Yield Healthy Behavior

In the same way that old, toxic mindsets produce a life of defeat, new mindsets produce a life of victory. Healthy beliefs yield healthy behavior. This was true in my own life. When I saw myself as a sinner, I acted like a sinner. When I saw myself as an Irish drunk, I got drunk. But when I saw myself as a redeemed and chosen child of God, I rose up to my new calling and purpose. My new beliefs produced new behaviors.

We see the same thing in the Apostle Peter's life. When he saw himself as a lewd, crude Galilean fisherman, he lived like a "sinful man" (Luke 5:8). When Jesus saved him and called him and filled him with the Holy Spirit, Peter had a dramatic change of mind. He no longer saw himself as a sinful man. He understood that he had a new identity in Christ. Peter now saw himself as part of a "chosen race, a royal priesthood, a holy nation, a people for his own possession," with a new calling of "proclaim[ing] the excellencies of him who called [him] out of darkness into his marvelous light" (1 Pet. 2:9). Peter's new beliefs produced new behaviors. With this new mindset, Peter went on to become one of the greatest leaders the church has ever known.

My friend Jake is another example of someone who completely changed his beliefs about himself. There was a time in his life when he believed he was a chronic failure. He told me that he was so depressed he couldn't get out of bed. He lost his job and was abusing various substances. In this pit of despair, God sent a ray of light. Jake started listening to an online preacher. Every morning, he would wake up to the powerful, faith-filled words of this man's preaching. It changed Jake's life. He began to believe again, and instead of looking at himself as a chronic failure, he believed and confessed that he was a new creature in Christ. God did a transformational work in Jake's life, as his healthy beliefs produced healthy behaviors. He started working out again and got clean and sober. He joined a church and God gave him a much better job than he had before. Jake was finally living like the new creature he really was.

YOUR BELIEFS about your identity will produce a life of victory or a life of defeat. When you wake up every morning and put on your new identity in Christ, you will live a life of victory and fruitfulness in God's kingdom. I highly encourage you to go back several pages and read the list of forty-six Scripture affirmations, "Who I Am in Christ." Read these verses daily; internalize them; confess them with your mouth. They will sink deeply into your spirit and establish who you really are: a new creature in Christ!

Discussion Questions

1. Do you tend to see yourself as a new creature in Christ, or do you still see yourself as the 'old you'?
2. What is the biggest lie that the devil whispers to you about your identity? How can you counteract this?
3. Have you tried confessing who you are in Christ using a list of Scriptures like Joyce Meyer's list of forty-six truths, found in this chapter? If so, how did it affect you?
4. Read 2 Corinthians 5:17 and discuss what it means to you.

How can this verse become more of a reality in your daily life?

5. Since beliefs affect behavior, what are some of the new behaviors that come from your new identity in Christ?
6. What is one practical thing you can do this week to remind yourself of your new identity in Christ?

9
WATCH WHAT YOU EAT

"When you put the good, the clean, the pure, the powerful, and the positive into your mind, your life will dramatically improve."—Zig Ziglar

I HAVE a friend who runs triathlons. Training to swim 2.4 miles, bike 112 miles and run 26.2-miles in one race is an all-consuming endeavor. He has to buy the right gear, sleep more, massage his wrecked muscles, and be willing to wake up at 4:00 AM in the dead of winter to train before work. And he has to eat differently. He tells me that fueling his body for athletic training is almost as important as the training itself. Lots of lean protein, all-natural carbs and fruits and veggies are on the menu. He avoids garbage food, because every athlete knows the old adage: garbage in, garbage out. He spends countless hours honing his body for peak performance—he's not about to ruin his progress with a Big Mac and fries.

The lessons you learn in athletic training apply to your spiritual life as well. As Christians, we need to monitor our diets. We are all constantly feeding on something in the mental and spiritual realm.

What we allow into our eyes and ears, and consequently into our hearts and minds, has a major impact on our lives. When you fill yourself with garbage, it's very difficult to live a victorious life. When you feed on good spiritual food, however, you are much more likely to live the undefeated life.

David's Covenant With His Eyes

I love what David says in Psalm 101:2-3,

> "I will ponder the way that is blameless. Oh when will you come to me? I will walk with integrity of heart within my house; I will not set before my eyes anything that is worthless. I hate the work of those who fall away; it shall not cling to me."

David was determined to ponder, or focus his mind, on the way that is blameless. Like Job, David had made a covenant with his eyes to only look on things that would build his faith (Job 31:1). He was going to spend his days thinking godly thoughts. David knew the connection between thoughts and behavior. Even in the privacy of his house, when no one else was watching, David committed himself to not look at sin. He realized that what he allowed to fill his eyes would also fill his mind and eventually cling to his heart. When David broke this rule, and allowed his eyes to gaze on Bathsheba, he suffered dearly for his sin. His kingdom and his legacy were impacted for the rest of his life. It was a hard lesson, but David never forgot the truth of garbage in, garbage out. That's why he committed so strongly in this Psalm to never fill his mind with sinful thoughts. After repenting of his sin with Bathsheba, David made sure his mind never veered in that direction again. He fed on good spiritual food every morning, rising early to fill himself with praise and prayer and purpose.

What are you filling yourself with? Do you allow things that God hates to enter your eyes and ears on a daily basis? Of course, we all live in this crazy world and can't avoid all uncleanness. We would have to lock ourselves up in monasteries, and even then, we couldn't avoid the uncleanness of this world. I'm not talking about going through life with blinders on. We will hear curse words and see things that are ungodly—I get it. But we can choose the overall tone and tenor of our atmosphere. We are not helpless victims of this unclean world. We can wake up and say no to certain things, and yes to better things. We can close the door on the unclean and unhealthy and open it wide to the pure and the good.

Linda's Breakthrough

The problem is, when it comes to watching and listening to things that God hates, everybody else does it. We are surrounded by people who do it, and it doesn't seem to affect them for the worse. I would disagree, however, with that assessment. It does affect them, whether you realize it or not. Whatever we allow into our minds affect us. What we dwell on becomes our destiny. Linda came to me because she was suffering from terrible anxiety. It had gotten to the point where she had difficulty leaving the house. I prayed over her and ministered life to her, and then felt the Holy Spirit prompt me to ask her about her spiritual and mental diet. "What are you allowing into your mind on a consistent basis?" I asked.

"Well, I'm not too good at that, Pastor Dave," she said. "I admit that I watch a lot of ungodly stuff and the material I consume on the internet is not good for my mental health."

"That's your biggest problem then," I said. "You need to decrease the negative input and increase the positive input. Whatever you put into your mind will come out one way or another. If you want peace, you need to feed on peace. If you want joy, you have to fill yourself with joy."

"OK, Pastor Dave," Linda said. "But how do I do that?"

"It's not hard," I said. "Get a jump on the negativity by rising early and filling yourself with praise and prayer. Let the Word of God be the first thing on your mind. And then, when the devil comes knocking, don't answer the door. On your commute, listen to something faith-building. As often as you can, put on praise music. As you change your atmosphere, your mind will change, and as your mind changes, your walk will change. You will walk in victory like never before." Linda took my advice, and the change I see in her is remarkable. She is now confident, happy and faith-filled.

"My only regret is that I didn't start living this way years ago!" she recently told me. "Why I filled my mind with all that garbage, I don't know. It was definitely dragging me down. I have so much peace now, it's ridiculous!" Just like Linda, you can choose to make a change in your spiritual diet. When you change what you consume, you change what you exude. When Linda fed on junk, anxiety and fear came out of her. As she consumed the pure spiritual food of the Word, peace and confidence exuded from her.

I Can Handle It

Sometimes people disagree with my stance on avoiding worldly junk in their spiritual diet. "I can handle it, Pastor Dave," they say. "It's just a little cursing, a little nudity, a little false religion, a little uncleanness." My problem is often you think you are handling it, but it's handling you. It's getting into you and diminishing your spiritual fire and blunting the edge of your faith. There are times in life when a little bit is too much. This was perfectly illustrated by a preacher I once saw in Dallas, Texas. He brought a blender and a can of Pepsi on stage for his sermon illustration. He held up the can of soda and said, "Who would like to drink this ice-cold soda on this hot day?" A lot of hands went up. He poured the soda into the blender and said, "OK, just one more thing. I have a couple of small items to add to the soda before I give it you. This is half of a cockroach I found in my hotel this morning. This is a bit of used tissue I found on the floor in the restroom. And this is a bit of dog poop I found on the sidewalk." He threw the items into the blender and turned it on. After a few seconds, he stopped the blender and poured the contents into a tall glass. "Alright, who's first?" he said as he held up the glass. As you can imagine, there were no takers. "Then why," he asked, "do we put up with just a little sin and uncleanness in our spiritual lives? Why do we excuse our sin and come to God as if we are all clean? Sometimes a little bit is too much."

In the same way that drinking soda with a little bit of poop is gross, a Christian mind with a little bit of uncleanness is gross. You were made for better. You were made to be filled with purity and faith and truth and light. Don't allow the junk of the world to dim your light.

Negative Nancy

The cool thing is this: you have the power to choose the tenor of your atmosphere. You choose what your mind will dwell on. You choose what you allow to enter your eyes and ears. Your power to choose is an incredible power. I used to work with a negative Nancy. Her name actually was Nancy, and I'm convinced the term "negative Nancy" was coined because of her. Every day when I arrived to work, she was there with a fresh complaint. She thrived on negativity. She took a sick delight in pointing out all that was wrong in the world, and steadfastly refused to listen to the slightest bit of positivity. No sir—it had to be negative or she wouldn't hear it.

Nancy's negativity was like a toxic slime that oozed out of her and filled the office. One day, I realized that her slime was beginning to affect me. I was stepping in it every morning, and it was clinging to my shoes. I was bringing it home from work. Some of my viewpoints were getting slimy. "Oh my goodness, I hate that lousy politician," I complained to my wife one afternoon.

"Well, we can't change that, so we might as well be happy," Raquel replied.

"Can't change it? Be happy? Good grief, that attitude is the reason we are in this mess!"

"What mess, Dave?" she said. "I think the mess is in your mind." Ouch. I wasn't ready to receive the truth of this statement right away, but upon reflection, I realized that my wife had dropped a major truth bomb on me. The mess was in my mind! I was choosing to allow negative thinking to infect my mind, and it was coming out of me in ways that were affecting my family. The same might be true for you—the mess is in your mind. Yes, there are lousy politicians and unfair realities and negative coworkers and mean relatives and unforeseen challenges, but the outer mess doesn't have to become the inner mess, unless we allow it into our minds. In all these things, we are more than conquerors, if we learn to fill our minds with the peace and power of God's Word.

I made a decision to stop stepping in Nancy's negative slime. Whatever she said, that was her thinking, not mine. I needed to get her mess out of my head, so I started rehearsing the promises of God every morning. I made the decision to change my spiritual diet. I woke up and spent time worshipping God and encouraging myself in the Lord. My tired spirit opened up like a flower to the sunshine. Now, before I got to work, I was filled with faith and joy. When I got to work and Nancy started spewing slime again, I tried a new technique. I began to bluntly confront her with positivity.

"Yeah but things always work out . . . God will make a way where there is no way . . . It can only get better from here." After several weeks of this, Nancy gave me one of the best compliments I've ever received. In the midst of one her rants, she mumbled to another coworker, "Don't bother mentioning that stuff to Dave. He's Mr. Positive now." Mr. Positive, I will take that moniker any day! I would so much rather be called Mr. Positive than Mr. Depressed or Mr. Morose or Mr. Bad Vibes. Wouldn't you?

Rise Up Like an Eagle

One time I was walking in the woods with my kids. It was a beautiful morning and we were enjoying the discoveries of the winding trail. All of sudden, my son Brandon, who had run ahead, shouted, "Hey Dad, you have to see this!" As the rest of us turned the corner, we saw what he was referring to: a majestic bald eagle perched on a fencepost twenty yards away. We all froze in wonder as it spread its broad wings and lifted up in flight, slowly soaring over the field that adjoins the woods.

"Wow," I said, "that was a bald eagle, guys!" Later that morning, we stumbled upon a very different scene: a group of turkey vultures hunched over the carcass of a dead animal.

"Look Daddy, more *eeglas*," my daughter said.

"Those aren't eeglas, Sweety," I said. "Those are vultures. Eagles don't eat dead animals—only vultures do." It made me think about how different these birds are. When I got home that day, I looked it up, and it turns out that eagles and vultures are both in the Accipitridae family, but their diets are very different. Eagles will only eat what they catch, but vultures love to scavenge for dead animals. Eagles feed on life—vultures feed on death. The same is true of Christians. Those who want to grow their faith feed on life. They are careful to monitor what comes into their minds and they are intentional about filling themselves with good spiritual food. They are eagles.

The Bible says that those "who wait for the Lord shall renew their strength; they shall mount up with wings like *eagles*" (Isa. 40:31, emphasis added). According to God, you are an eagle, not a vulture. God wants you to soar above the junk and the negativity with wings like an eagle. You are not called to rub shoulders with the buzzards around carcasses of death. You are called to soar. But in order to fly, you have to watch your diet. You must be careful to feed on life, just like the eagle. You must be selective about what you consume mentally and spiritually, because you are an eagle. Wouldn't it be absurd to see a bald eagle in a circle of turkey vultures, picking at a dead carcass? "Lift up your wings and fly out of there, eagle!" you would say. "You were made for better."

In the same way, it's absurd to see Christians feeding on worldly junk that only contaminates the soul. You are an eagle—you were made for better than that. When an eagle takes off from the ground, it flaps its wings three or four times and then stops flapping and starts soaring. It rides the thermal updrafts and soars above everything below.

What a beautiful picture of the Christian life. It doesn't matter what is happening below. Be an eagle and soar above the ungodliness that permeates our society. Don't let the vultures pull you down—spread your wings and soar on the winds of the Spirit.

Positive Technology

One of the greatest advantages of our technological age is that now we all have mini-computers in our hands. With our smartphones, we can access all kinds of great content any time of day. From sermon podcasts to the audio Bible, we can watch and listen to positive, faith-building material that will stir the fire in our souls and keep the devil under our feet. When I am at the gym, I typically run on the treadmill for forty-five minutes, which is the perfect amount of time to listen to a sermon or a leadership podcast. My life has been enriched and my leadership enhanced by this one simple habit. Every morning as my wife gets ready for work, she listens to the One Year Bible on audio. It's the greatest thing in the world to hear the fresh, powerful Word of God when I walk into the room. Our smartphones have the ability to change our atmospheres for the better, if we seek out good content and fill ourselves with it daily.

Jeremy came to me when he was in crisis. "I messed up, Pastor Dave," he said. "I've been in recovery from heroin addiction, but I relapsed." I jumped in and helped Jeremy through the detox process and then enrolled him in a three-month treatment program. He ended up staying there for nine months and came out a new man. Jeremy has been clean for several years now, and I recently had coffee with him. I wanted to ask him one question. Knowing the relapse rate of heroin addicts, I wanted to find out what Jeremy's secret was. How was he managing to soar above the temptation that pulls so many others down, right back to the dead carcasses of addiction? How was he managing to beat the odds and stay clean?

"You've been clean for a number of years now, Jeremy," I said. "In that time, you have seen two of your old friends die from drug overdoses."

"Three," he interrupted.

"Wow, three," I said. "But you have stayed clean. Every time I see you, you are full of faith, you've got a smile on your face, you've always got a positive word to say. What's your secret?"

"Well, besides going to meetings and staying away from my old crowd, my number one secret is right here," Jeremy said, holding up his smartphone.

"What do you mean?" I asked. I thought he meant that a friend called him regularly on the phone to encourage him.

"It's all about what you feed your mind, Pastor Dave," he said.

"You mean that you listen to positive content on your smartphone?" I said. "Tell me more."

"Well, every morning I have breakfast with Joel," he replied. After seeing the quizzical look on my face, he continued, "As I eat breakfast, I listen to a sermon from Joel Osteen. His positive faith always charges me up for the day and sets my mind on the Word. Then I listen to Christian music while I'm sitting on the bus. The songs of faith always lift my spirit. When I get home from work, I listen to the audio Bible. God's pure and powerful Word challenges me, convicts me and comforts me. I am feeding myself all day long with good stuff, so the bad stuff has no place in me!"

Just like Jeremy, you need to fill yourself with good stuff. If you have a smartphone, use it to fill your mind and heart with sermons, podcasts, songs and teachings from God's Word. You will be so full of the good stuff, that the bad stuff will have no place in you. Before long, you will be walking in faith and victory instead of discouragement and defeat.

Filling Your Mind

The Apostle Paul monitored his spiritual diet closely. He knew the truth of the principle, 'garbage in, garbage out.' He also knew the truth of 'Jesus is, Jesus out.' He saw that when he focused his mind on things that were true and noble, he was filled with faith and power. That's why he ends his letter to the Philippians this way: "Summing it all up, friends, I'd say you'll do best by filling your minds and meditating on things true, noble, reputable, authentic, compelling, gracious—the best, not the worst; the beautiful, not the ugly; things to praise, not things to curse" (Phil 4:8 MSG). Watch your spiritual diet, Paul was saying. Fill your mind with good things, and you will walk in victory. Fill your mind with the world's garbage, and you will walk in defeat. Paul believed that your destiny is tied to your thought life.

Did you know that the average person has 10,000 separate thoughts each day? Every one of those 10,000 thoughts is a choice you intentionally make to think about one thing and not another. Imagine someone gave you $10,000 and said, "Spend it any way you like, as long as you spend it all before going to bed tonight." You'd be careful how you spent the money, wouldn't you? We should exercise the same care over the thoughts we think. Ralph Waldo Emerson said, "Beware of what you set your mind on because that you surely will become."[1] Your destiny is tied to your thought life, and you have the choice to focus your mind on positive truth or allow it to wander into the morass of negativity. Like Paul, I would say that you'd do best by filling your mind with things that build your faith, keep your heart pure and light your soul on fire for Jesus.

In the years before he became a follower of Christ, Paul had filled his mind with unclean things. When we first meet him in Acts 9, he is a man filled with anger, unbelief, conflict and arrogance. He spent his time raging against believers in Jesus, imprisoning them and even killing them. Because his mind was unclean, his entire life was unclean. And then a miracle happened: God saved Paul. In one day, his entire life turned around. His soul and his spirit were cleansed and freed from his old sinful ways. But Paul's mind wasn't cleansed in one day. Even though his spirit was free, his mind had the tendency to return to its old ways. Paul found that, if he wasn't careful, old thoughts would try to drag him down and hold him back.

The Mind Dwells on What You Feed It

Paul had a choice to make. Either he was going to allow his mind to hold him back, or he was going to figure out how to get his mind under control and keep moving forward. That's when he made the discovery of a lifetime. The mind simply dwells on whatever you feed it. Paul explains this truth in Romans 8,

> "For those who live according to the flesh set their minds on the things of the flesh, but those who live according to the Spirit set their minds on the things of the Spirit. For to set the mind on the flesh is death, but to set the mind on the Spirit is life and peace" (vs 5-6).

Paul said to himself, "I'm going to live in life and peace, so from this day forward, I choose to never be a victim of my own mind again. I choose to fill my mind with things that are true, noble, reputable, authentic, compelling and gracious." Because Paul made this choice to constantly feed his mind good spiritual food, he lived in constant victory. Nothing could get him down—not beatings, not imprisonments, not shipwrecks. He would say,

> "If God is for us, who can be against us? . . . Who shall separate us from the love of Christ? Shall tribulation, or distress, or persecution, or famine, or nakedness, or danger, or sword? . . . No, in all these things we are more than conquerors through him who loved us" (Rom 8:31,35,37).

YOU CAN HAVE the same attitude as Paul. In the face of your shipwrecks, you can be faith-filled and victorious. I have attempted to have this attitude for the past thirty years. Every time I face a setback or a letdown, I think of Paul saying, "Will this separate us from the love of Christ? No! We are more than conquerors in Christ!" As I fill my mind with good spiritual food from God's Word, there is no room for the junk, and it is much easier for me to stay in faith. I challenge you to do the same thing: consistently fill your mind with good spiritual food. Be diligent to weed out the junk. Make God's promises your daily meditation, and the undefeated life will be yours.

Discussion Questions

1. How would you describe your current spiritual diet? What do allow into your eyes and ears on a regular basis?
2. Describe a time when you watched something or listened to something and it affected your spirit or your mood negatively.
3. Read Philippians 4:8 and Romans 8:5-6 and share how you can live out these verses in your life.
4. What is one thing you can remove from your mental or spiritual diet that will help you stay in peace and walk in faith?
5. What is one thing you can add to your mental or spiritual diet that will help you stay in peace and walk in faith?

10

WIN THE WAR

"Warfare happens every day, all the time. Whether you believe it or not, you are in a battlefield. You are in warfare."—Pedro Okoro

"You are not fighting for victory—you are fighting from victory. This battle has already been won!"—Tony Evans

THE CHRISTIAN LIFE IS A WAR, not a picnic. If you are going to succeed as a follower of Jesus, you must learn to fight. Living the undefeated life requires you to resist the enemy and enforce the victory that Jesus has already won.

So many Christians are weak and tentative in their faith. The devil loves that attitude. It's not time to back down or sit down in the battle— it's time to stand and fight! We need less, "Oh God, if you could maybe spare a tiny little blessing for me," and more, "Thank you Lord that your Word declares that I am the head and not the tail and you have given me every spiritual blessing in heavenly places in Christ." God has called you to fight the good fight of faith, not crumble at the first sign of resistance. Be on guard—your faith will be weak and tentative if you fall into any of these three categories:

Your Faith Will Be Weak If . . .

1. **You want to be liked.** Your calling is not to be accepted and liked by everyone around you. Jesus wants you to stand out, not fit in. He said, "If the world hates you, keep in mind that it hated me first. If you belonged to the world, it would love you as its own. As it is, you do not belong to the world, but I have chosen you out of the world. That is why the world hates you" (John 15:18-19 NIV). Your calling is to live for Jesus and show Him to the world. This will mean that some people will oppose you and misunderstand you. Don't buckle. Stand firm in your faith and keep representing Jesus with a smile.
2. **You don't know the Word.** When the promises of God are ready on your tongue, the devil is on the run. Your faith weakens when you let the Word dwindle in your memory and in your mouth. Yesterday's Word is not enough—what is God saying to you today? I encourage you to arrange your day so God's promises retain a prominent place in your mind. You can use Bible study, devotional books, worship music, smartphone apps—whatever works for you. "This Book of the Law shall not depart from your mouth. . .and then you will have good success" (Josh 1:8).
3. **You don't feed your faith.** You can't go into battle and succeed if you haven't eaten in a week. A strong faith requires a steady diet of spiritual food. Sporadic Christians have sporadic victories. If you want to live the undefeated life, you need to feed your faith daily. "And they *devoted* themselves to the apostles' teaching and the fellowship, to

the breaking of bread and the prayers." (Acts 2:42, emphasis mine).

Stand and Fight

Don't lose your fighting spirit. I remember a time when I almost lost mine. I was in a season of life when things were not going well at work. Every day was a challenge. I felt empty, frustrated and angry. I knew that God had called me to this position years earlier, but the grace was now wearing off. Then I got overlooked for a promotion. How about a zero percent raise for another year of torment? Yay, sign me up! When I got home that day, I had a little talk with God. "I'm done, Lord," I said. "I'm just so *tired*. I try to live for you 100%, but it's like you don't back me up sometimes. I want out of this job."

"Stand up," I heard the Holy Spirit speak to my heart.

"Come again?" I said. Again, I felt that God was telling me to stand up. I was seated on my couch, so I grudgingly stood up. I began to pace the floor, still complaining to the Lord. Before long, God interrupted my tirade with a distinct impression to open my Bible to Ephesians 6.

> "Put on the full armor of God, so that you can take your *stand* against the devil's schemes. For our struggle is not against flesh and blood, but against the rulers, against the authorities, against the powers of this dark world and against the spiritual forces of evil in the heavenly realms. Therefore put on the full armor of God, so that when the day of evil comes, you may be able to *stand* your ground, and after you have done everything, to *stand*. *Stand* firm then (Eph 6:11-14 NIV, emphasis mine).

Four times in just four verses, Paul exhorts us to stand. I realized that I was not standing my ground in the spiritual battle. I was letting the enemy invade my head with depression and despair. I was seated when I should have been standing. No one else could stand up for me. I had to do it. I saw it so clearly—if I remained seated, the enemy was going to take more and more ground. It was time to stand up, shake off the weight, and begin to push back. God had called me, and where God guides, He provides. God was surely going to honor my faithfulness and obedience, even if there were dark seasons I needed to pass through. Better days were coming—I just needed to stand!

When my wife asked me how work went that day, I said, "It's all good. God has great things in store for us!"

"Amen," she replied, not knowing that I almost quit one hour earlier. The next day, I got called into my boss's office. "Sorry about the delay, but here is your updated compensation package." I read the letter and was amazed to see that I had received a raise after all. It wasn't much, but it was enough. "Thank you, God, for teaching me to stand," I thought as I left that office with a big smile on my face.

Battle Tactics

The Christian life is a battle, but with God's help, you can win. You can live undefeated. Over the years, I have learned some hard-won battle tactics, and I want to share them with you in this chapter. First, let me lay a few ground rules about using these battle tactics:

1. **They are not just for special saints.** Anyone can win the spiritual war, not just the specially-gifted or spiritually-advanced. If you believe in the veracity of God's Word and know how to pray, you can win. Don't let the devil intimidate you. He is a defeated foe. You are fighting from a place of victory, not struggling to win a victory yourself. You are an enforcer of what Jesus has already done. You are a maintainer of Jesus' absolute victory over sin and death through His completed work on the cross and His resurrection from the dead. You have the full authority of the King behind you. Use it!
2. **You must use them constantly.** The devil doesn't take days off. The spiritual conflict in which we are engaged is daily,

constant and lifelong. Yes, there are beautiful seasons of rest, but we never fully disengage from the battle. That time will come in heaven. Until then, we fight. We wake up and resist the world, the flesh and the devil. We ask God to cover us in the blood and fill us with the Spirit. We fight daily, not sporadically, because sporadic Christians get sporadic victories.

3. **No yelling is necessary.** Spiritual warfare is not about volume, it's about faith. The devil fears the one who clings to God's Word more than the one who hoots and hollers. It's about standing in faith, not waving your sword in a silly show of strength. If you can stand and believe God when the wind is in your face, you will win the battle. The style of your singing or praying is irrelevant—it's your fearless faith that counts.

Now, let's jump in and look at the seven battle tactics for winning the spiritual war. I encourage you to focus on one tactic per day over the next week.

Seven Battle Tactics for Winning the Spiritual War:

ONE: The name. Jesus Christ is the name above all names, and the devil knows it. In all your prayers, in all your petitions, in all your praises, the name of Jesus should have preeminence. Invoking the name of a prominent person implies that I have the permission and the authority of that person. If I say to you, "I come in the name of the President," you will immediately treat me differently. I will have authority that no one else in the room has. I will get things done that no one else can, because I come in the name of the President. Jesus Christ, God's only son, gave you His permission and His authority when He said, "Whatever you ask in my name, this I will do, that the Father may be glorified in the Son" (John 14:13). In other words, "Use my name!"

When I was new to the faith and still learning about spiritual warfare, I learned an unforgettable lesson one afternoon by taking a nap. I woke up with a start, and there was something on top of me, but it wasn't human. It was some kind of spiritual force, and it was stopping me from breathing. Ah, the adventures of napping! Needless to say, I freaked out. I screamed, "Get off me!" Nothing happened. I yelled, "God help me!" Again, nothing happened. Finally, in desperation, I shouted the one name, the only name that can save, "Jesus!" Immediately the evil force left me. Like a mist, it disappeared. I drew in a long breath and lay there in shock for a moment. "Whoo, what just happened?" I thought.

God wanted to imprint something on my mind that I would never forget. Prayers are good, praises are good, but there is nothing like the name of Jesus Christ. He literally has the name "that is above every name" (Phil 2:9). As Peter explained to the crowd after God miraculously healed the lame beggar,

> "By faith in the name of Jesus, this man whom you see and know was made strong. It is Jesus' name and the faith that comes through him that has completely healed him, as you can all see" (Acts 3:16).

If you are facing a spiritual battle, depend on the power of the name!

TWO: The blood. There is no force in the universe more powerful than the blood of Jesus. The blood represents the most important event in all of history: the cross of Jesus Christ, where sin was forever paid for and the devil was forever defeated. When God's innocent Son shed His blood for our sins, the enemy's hold on humanity was broken. He no longer has any legal right to rule over those who are in Christ. In all your spiritual struggles, you need to be reminding the enemy of the cross and the blood. That is where your freedom was purchased, and that is where your freedom is renewed every day.

On one of my trips to Mexico City, I visited an impoverished area with two pastor friends of mine. "This area is known for drugs, prostitution and crime," Enrique told me. "But they need Jesus, so that's why we come here." Just then, a young, shirtless man approached us and started yelling obscenities. He was erratic and incoherent, and he wouldn't leave us alone. Before long, other young men began to approach us as well, attracted by the commotion.

I began to pray, "Lord, I thank you for the blood of Jesus. I thank you that your blood is more powerful than any tactic of the enemy, as your Word declares, 'And they have conquered him by the blood of the Lamb and by the word of their testimony,' (Rev 12:11). I pray that you cover us in the blood of Jesus right now, and I pray that you also cover these young men in your blood and draw them to yourself."

It's rare that God answers my prayers immediately. Usually there is a wait time between the prayer and the answer. This was not one of those times. As soon as I finished praying, something changed. The young man stopped yelling and his demeanor softened. Enrique engaged him in conversation, and he responded with calmness and openness. Sensing an opportune moment, Enrique boldly announced to the gathering crowd, "We are here to share God's love with all of you," and proceeded to share the Gospel with them. We ended up having church on that little dirt road, and a number of people were saved and set free!

THREE: The Word. Jesus, our greatest example, fought many spiritual battles. I find it fascinating that He didn't call down legions of angels in His moments of need. He didn't snap His fingers and cast lightning bolts upon His enemies. Nope. Instead, He said, "It is written" (Matt 4:4). Those three words must be part of your vocabulary if you want to live the undefeated life.

It is written. Not, "Google says," or "Facebook says," but "God says." As an old preacher used to say, "God said it, I believe it, that settles it." We need to get better at hiding God's Word in our hearts and wielding it like a sword in our spiritual struggles.

Years ago, I had what I now know was an anxiety attack. Layer after layer of pressure from work and church and kids simply overwhelmed me, and I crashed. In my desperation, I ran to the only place I knew to go: the Word of God. "Lord, I need a word, *please* speak to me," I prayed, as I paced my office floor, Bible in hand. The Lord brought a verse to my mind that I hadn't thought of in years: "You keep him in perfect peace whose mind is stayed on you, because he trusts in you" (Isa. 26:3). A calmness entered my soul as I meditated on the implications of this verse. "So all I have to do," I said, "is keep my mind stayed on God. The best way I know to do that is by memorizing His Word!"

I went to the Bible book store (remember those?) on the way home from work and bought a Bible memory system. It contained sixty small cards, each with one verse on it. I carried my little cards with me wherever I went, and had the first six verses memorized after a week. It's not an overstatement to say that those little cards changed my life. I began to quote God's powerful, anointed Word in my struggles, and peace returned to my life. The tide shifted and I started to have more good days than bad. And while I still face anxiety at times, I have never returned to the pit I was in before discovering the power of, "It is written."

FOUR: Prayer. Wouldn't it be great to have a place of refuge, a place of peace, a place of comfort in the battle? Your prayer room is that place. God promises to make you lie down in green pastures, lead you beside still waters and restore your soul in the place of prayer (Psa. 23:2-3). Don't skip the blessing by skipping the place of prayer. Slow down and schedule time with God. David had his tent of prayer on the battlefield. Even when the battle was raging outside, he could say, "I will fear no evil, for you are with me" (Psa 23:4). When David was surrounded by enemies, his attitude was, "It's all good—God is on our side!" Time after time, God came through for David. David lived undefeated because David lived in the place of prayer.

I remember facing a time of heaviness in my life. Nothing in particular was wrong, but I felt down. So I prayed, but I didn't really pray, you know what I mean? I prayed a bit in the car and a bit in the shower, but I was skipping my place of prayer, where I really met with God. I was a busy man, after all. So the heaviness persisted. I came home from work after a couple of weeks of this, and I felt so frustrated that I locked myself in my room. When my wife texted me to come down for dinner, I replied, "Not until God sets me free." Dramatic, I know. But I needed God. I prayed. I cried. I worshipped. And guess what? After thirty or forty minutes, God set me free. I'm convinced that certain prayers need to pass the thirty minute mark before the blessing comes. There is something powerful about praying until you get a breakthrough. The old timers used to call it 'praying through.' If you need a blessing, don't stop praying until you have 'prayed through,' and you sense a release. We spend three hours watching a ball game—why can't we spend thirty uninterrupted minutes worshipping God and praying?

FIVE: Tongues. One of the greatest blessings in my life is the prayer language I received when I was baptized in the Holy Spirit on October 25, 1990. Since that time, not a single day has passed without me using this wonderful gift of speaking in tongues. Don't get hung up on the fact that speaking in tongues seems weird to you—let God be God and embrace all that He has for you.

After rising from the dead, Jesus told His disciples that a special blessing was coming soon, and instructed them "not to depart from Jerusalem, but to wait for the promise of the Father, which, he said, 'you heard from me; for John baptized with water, but you will be baptized with the Holy Spirit not many days from now'" (Acts 1:4-5). The disciples gathered in the upper room and prayed and worshiped until the Holy Spirit showed up! Exactly what Jesus predicted happened, and "they were all filled with the Holy Spirit and began to speak in other tongues as the Spirit gave them utterance." (Acts 2:4). This amazing empowerment turned these ordinary men and women into powerhouses for God. Here is the clincher: this same power is available today. Nowhere in the Bible does it say God is going to stop pouring out His Holy Spirit and empowering believers with supernatural giftings. Why wouldn't you want all that God has for you? For detailed information on how to receive the baptism in the Holy Spirit, please visit www.cfn.org/literature/ and download the free pdf booklet.

One of the greatest benefits of speaking in tongues is that the Spirit of God will pray through you when you don't know how to pray for (Rom. 8:26-27). How many times have you hit a wall in your prayer time, when your human understanding has reached its limit, and you don't know how to pray? That's when praying in tongues comes in! The Spirit of God knows exactly what to pray for, so God uses your voice and your cooperation with the Holy Spirit to bring about the perfect prayer.

I was once on a street outreach in the Deep Ellum section of Dallas, Texas. A group of students and I were singing worship songs and talking to people about Jesus. I noticed one young man who was seated on the curb, staring at us with a blank look on his face. I went over and tried to talk to him, but he just growled at me. "Interesting response," I thought, and began to pray silently for him. I had no idea what to pray for, so I prayed in tongues. Just then, the word, "abuse" flashed in my mind. I trusted the leading of the Holy Spirit, and went back over to the young man and sat down next to him.

"Life is hard, man," I said, "full of abuse and people mistreating us." It was like I'd hit him in the head with a two by four. He swung around and looked at me, eyes opened wide, and said, "How the heck did you know that?" It was an amazing moment. God had revealed to me, through the gift of praying in tongues, exactly what this young man was struggling with, and it opened his heart to talk to us about God. He ended up receiving Christ as his Lord and Savior that night, and started coming to church with us on Sundays!

SIX: Praise. If you have not yet learned to praise God in your valleys, then praise is your missing key to victory. I have learned that there is no victory apart from praise. Praise opens the windows of heaven and shuts the door on the devil. Praise gives you strength when you're weary. Praise is the wind in your sails. Praise is the sunrise on the morning dew. I suppose you could live without it, but why would you want to?

Paul and Silas learned the power of praise when their hands and feet were bound in stocks in the Philippian jail (Acts 16). Their bodies couldn't move, but their tongues could praise. Around midnight, when they should have been sleeping from exhaustion, they were singing praise songs. They weren't whispering old hymns in the corner, they were singing Gospel tunes at the top of their lungs. God was so good, in spite of their trials, that they had to praise Him! Other prisoners began to notice, and I think some of them began to sing along. God was so pleased by their praise that He gave all of the prisoners "Get out of jail free" cards. He sent an earthquake that shook the prison doors open, and all the prisoners instantly became ex-prisoners. The power of praise!

I have a friend who says that praise saved her life. She found herself in a dark valley after she caught her fiancé cheating on her and had to cancel the wedding at the last minute. She sank so low that she planned to kill herself. She wrote the suicide note, left it on her kitchen counter, and walked out of her house with a bottle of pills. She walked down to the beach and sat alone on the sand, gazing at the ocean one last time before she took the pills. It was then that she heard something that made her look around. No one else was on the beach, but she heard music. She kept looking to see where the music was coming from, but she didn't see anybody. It was an old Phil Keaggy praise song called, "Sunday's Child." The lyrics spoke to her, especially the lines, "You will find no peace of mind / Til you're Sunday's child" and "While time is still on your side, / Take the love that is here." In her despair, a tiny ray of hope dawned. She sang along, and she cried. By the time the song finished, she looked down at the bottle of pills and thought, "What am I doing?" She made her way back home and called her mother, confessing everything that happened. Although she never found out who was playing that praise song, she can truly say that praise saved her life.

SEVEN: The prayers of others. My seventh and final battle tactic for winning the spiritual war is one that I neglected for years. I thought it was a nice bonus to have others pray for me, but certainly not essential. Now I know better. Having others in your corner that are actively praying for you is often the key difference between success and failure. The battle is just too intense to fight alone. We need one another, and not in a casual way ("Hey bro, I will keep you in prayer"). You need to be on someone's daily prayer list. You need someone to fight for you in prayer intentionally and consistently.

There is one thing you have to do in order to activate this battle tactic: you must tell somebody your needs, and ask them to pray for you. Don't miss out on this incredible blessing because you are afraid to open your life a bit and share your struggles. Even the great Apostle Paul asked others to pray for him on at least three separate occasions (Rom. 15:30-32, Eph. 6:19-20, Col. 4:3-4). Find one or two people who you trust and ask them to pray for you!

One time I was leading a group of twenty students on a missions trip to the Dominican Republic. Unexpectedly, one of the students fell dangerously ill. We were far from home, but we just happened to be across the street from a medical clinic at the time. I rushed the student into the clinic, and the receptionist told me, "Sorry, but the doctor has gone home for the day." As we were speaking, a doctor walked into the hallway, and the receptionist said, "Oh, there you are, doctor. I thought you had left already. Could you have a look at this patient?" The doctor administered immediate care to my student which likely saved his life, and we left the clinic, greatly relieved, after about an hour.

When we returned home to New Jersey, we had a meeting with all the students and their parents. I told stories of what the Lord had done, including the story about the doctor appearing at just the right time, with just the right medical care for our student. One of the moms raised her hand and asked, "On what day did that happen?" I told her that it happened on Tuesday and her eyes widened. "At what time?" she asked. When I told her it happened at around 11:00 AM, she gasped. "I attend a weekly prayer meeting on Tuesday mornings at 10:00 AM, and while you were on the trip, I felt particularly burdened to pray for divine protection and miraculous healing. I thought it was for the Dominican people, but little did I know that God was having me pray for our own team." Prayer works!

USE these seven battle tactics to win your own spiritual war. The devil wants to discourage you and demoralize you. Don't let him! Stand up and use the Name of Jesus, plead the blood over your life, believe in and confess the Word, pray without ceasing, pray in tongues, never stop praising Jesus and solicit the help of others to pray for you. Remember, I am praying for you as you read this book that victory will be yours!

Discussion Questions

1. Describe your current involvement in the spiritual battle. How engaged are you in the battle, from not-at-all to fully-immersed?
2. Which one of the Seven Battle Tactics do you find compelling, and why?
3. Read 2 Corinthians 10:3-4 and share how you can live out these verses in your life.
4. What is one change you can make to become more engaged in the spiritual battle?
5. Which one of the Seven Battle Tactics can you focus on this week, and how?

11

YOUR SECRET WEAPON

"The Spirit-filled life is not a special, deluxe edition of Christianity. It is part and parcel of the total plan of God for His people."—A.W. Tozer

THE SECRET WEAPON to living the undefeated life is the Holy Spirit. God gave us a source of power and victory and wisdom and guidance: His Spirit. When we ignore this and look elsewhere, we fail. When we raise our sails and catch the wind of the Holy Spirit, the Christian life becomes a truly joyful experience.

When I was newly converted to Christ in 1990, I didn't know the power of the Holy Spirit. As I read the pages of Scripture, I saw that there must be more to the Christian life. Why do I see believers being filled with the Holy Spirit, speaking in tongues and prophesying in the New Testament, but nothing is happening in my own life? That was unacceptable to me. "I want the whole package, God," I said.

It was about that time that a book fell into my hands that changed my life. It was a little blue volume with colorful flames on the cover titled, *They Speak With Other Tongues*. The book chronicles author John Sherrill's journey from skeptic to investigator to believer in the Baptism in the Holy Spirit. Sherrill presented his case in such a level-headed and balanced way that I was highly intrigued. "That sounds like something I need," I thought. But first, I had to get clarity on exactly what the Bible teaches about the Baptism in the Holy Spirit.

Back to the Book

It turns out the Bible is crystal clear on this subject. The Old Testament prophesies it, Jesus predicts it, the Father sends it, and all those who are in Christ have the privilege of receiving it. God has always intended for believers to be Spirit-filled and Spirit-led.

A particularly compelling series of verses occurs from Luke 24 to Acts 2 (both written by Luke). Jesus is hanging out with His disciples in Luke 24. He has already risen from the dead, and He is about to go back to heaven, so He wants to give them some final instructions.

> "Then he said to them, 'These are my words that I spoke to you while I was still with you, that everything written about me in the Law of Moses and the Prophets and the Psalms must be fulfilled.' Then he opened their minds to understand the Scriptures, and said to them, 'Thus it is written, that the Christ should suffer and on the third day rise from the dead, and that repentance for the forgiveness of sins should be proclaimed in his name to all nations, beginning from Jerusalem. You are witnesses of these things. And behold, I am sending the promise of my Father upon you. But stay in the city until you are clothed with power from on high'" (Luke 24:44-49).

Jesus is saying, "OK here's the deal guys. You are going to launch the Christian Church into the world. Your main job is to preach the Gospel. But don't miss this one thing: I have a very special gift for you. Go to Jerusalem and wait there until you receive it." What would you do? Would you say, "Nah, we're good, Jesus. We can do church without your special gift." Never! You would clear your schedule and run to that Upper Room and wait there with excitement and expectancy. So why do we ignore the Holy Spirit in today's church? We will come back to this question in a moment.

Jesus' Last Words

In Acts 1, Luke records the final moments that Jesus was on this earth. What was the last thing that He said? You would assume that His final words would be very important. They probably aren't going to be, "Hey Peter, make sure you grab lunch for the guys after I'm gone" or "Hey, it's been real, guys—I'm out."

Jesus actually said, "You will receive power when the Holy Spirit has come upon you, and you will be my witnesses in Jerusalem and in all Judea and Samaria, and to the end of the earth" (Acts 1:8). In other words, "Remember the mission, guys, and don't forget where your power comes from!" If you were the Apostle John, would you ignore Jesus' last words? Would you go and try to plant churches in that hostile, pagan world with no thought to the one power source that Jesus mentions? So why do we ignore the Holy Spirit in today's church? Again, we will return to this question in a moment.

Not long after Jesus' ascension, 120 of His followers were huddled in the Upper Room on the Day of Pentecost, and something remarkable happened.

> "And suddenly there came from heaven a sound like a mighty rushing wind, and it filled the entire house where they were sitting. And divided tongues as of fire appeared to them and rested on each one of them. And they were all filled with the Holy Spirit and began to speak in other tongues as the Spirit gave them utterance" (Acts 2:2-4).

This was the true birth of the Church! Everything before this led up to this moment. Before Pentecost, they had teaching; after Pentecost, they had power. From this day forward, the Church was unstoppable. It spread rapidly through the nations, and by the year 200 AD, there were 250,000 followers of Jesus in the world. By the year 330

AD, Christianity was the dominant religion in the whole Roman Empire.

One thing I can tell you: the original leaders of the Christian church did not ignore the secret weapon of the Holy Spirit. They welcomed the Spirit, depended on the Spirit and rejoiced in the miracle-working power of the Spirit. Over and over again in the early church, we see the Holy Spirit empowering (Acts 4:31), supporting (Acts 5:32), speaking (Acts 13:2), deciding (Acts 15:28), directing (Acts 19:21) and prophesying (Acts 21:11). In just the Book of Acts, the Holy Spirit is mentioned fifty-six times!

If Jesus told you that He had a special gift for you, something designed just for you that would give you power and victory and joy, would you ignore it? Of course not—you would say, "Bring it on, Lord! I want that gift!" Yet, why do so many Christians try to live their lives as if the Holy Spirit doesn't exist? They might talk to the Father and talk to the Son, but they would never dream of talking to the Holy Spirit. Jesus gave them a gift, but it remains boxed up and wrapped up on the table.

Why Do We Ignore the Holy Spirit?

Why do we live our Christian lives as if there were no Holy Spirit? I can think of three reasons:

1. **Lack of knowledge.** Maybe you just don't know. No one ever told you about the Baptism in the Holy Spirit and the incredible power that comes with it. You have never done a Bible study on the work of the Holy Spirit in the believer's life. You have never witnessed someone praying in tongues or prophesying. When Paul first visited the city of Ephesus, he asked the believers if they had received the Holy Spirit. Their answer was astounding: "No, we have not even heard that there is a Holy Spirit" (Acts 19:2). Wow. Something so essential to the Christian faith, and they were completely oblivious to it. Paul immediately rectified the situation by

teaching them about the Baptism in the Holy Spirit, and "when Paul had laid his hands on them, the Holy Spirit came on them, and they began speaking in tongues and prophesying" (v 6).

2. **Denominational bias.** Certain Christian groups teach about the Baptism in the Holy Spirit, but only in the past tense. They tell you that one day it was real (in the days of the early church), but not anymore. For some inexplicable reason, God has stopped pouring out His Spirit and doing miracles today. How strange, because our world seems to be as desperately sick as it was in the days of the early church, and our need for power is the same or even greater. When I was a new Christian, I befriended a Baptist minister who told me in no uncertain terms that speaking in tongues was of the devil. "Well," I thought, "every day I pray in tongues and it leads me closer to Jesus, fills me with joy and empowers me to go and tell others about Christ. How can that be of the devil?" One time he asked me to pray for him, so we took hands and I began to pray. As I prayed, the Holy Spirit overflowed in tongues and my friend got a bit uncomfortable. But one week later, he came back to me and said, "God miraculously answered that prayer. Maybe there's something to that tongues stuff, after all!"

3. **Weird past experiences.** Perhaps you have seen Spirit-filled believers acting strangely. There are times when people claim something is from the Holy Spirit, but it's not. It's from their own flesh. They may have good intentions, but they are out of order. The solution is not to kick the Holy Spirit out of the church, but to curb the weirdness. Paul said, "Do not stifle the Holy Spirit. Do not scoff at prophecies, but test everything that is said. Hold on to what is good" (1 Thess. 5:19-21 NLT). Paul's rule for the churches was to embrace the supernatural, but make sure "all things [are] done decently and in order" (1 Cor. 14:40). I was in a church service once

when a woman stood up in the middle of the sermon and started giving a prophetic word. The pastor gently rebuked the woman by saying, "Dear sister, please hold that until later. Right now the Holy Spirit is speaking through the sermon, and God commands us to do all things decently and in order." The woman sat down and the sermon continued as planned. Was this woman malicious? No, she was just out of order. Don't let weirdness keep you from the Baptism in the Holy Spirit and the tremendous blessing it will bring to your life. Don't let the devil give you a skeptical heart and rob you of the gift of God. The Holy Spirit, as promised by Jesus Himself, will bring nothing but power and blessing into your life.

My Own Baptism

After becoming convinced that the Baptism in the Holy Spirit is both Biblical and highly-recommended for a full Christian life, I began to seek it. I prayed, I fasted, I cleansed my life of any leftover junk from my previous life. I was ready! On October 25, 1990, I was baptized in water at my church's Thursday night service. It was the most powerful, liberating and joyful night of my life. And it was about to get even better. As I was drying off and talking to my family in the front row, I noticed that my dad was talking to the pastor. They looked over at me and nodded.

"Oh boy," I thought, "I bet Dad just asked the pastor to pray over me to receive the Baptism in the Holy Spirit."

"You're all set," my dad said when he had walked back to us. "Pastor said to wait in his office." A thrill of excitement shot through me. Not long after I sat down in pastor's office, Pastor John and his wife Dot came in. Pastor John was the Associate Pastor, a genial white-haired man with a thick mustache and a thicker Brooklyn accent.

"I am so glad you are seeking the power from on high, David. Your life is about to change forever!" John beamed. With that, he opened his old leather Bible and read to me from Acts chapters 1 and 2. My heart was stirred and I was ready. Pastor John and Dot laid their hands on me and began to pray. I remember the beautiful lilting sound of Dot's heavenly language as she prayed in tongues over me. A surge of love entered me and I began to tremble.

"Go ahead and release your heavenly language, David," Pastor John said. I opened my mouth, and to my great surprise, I was speaking in tongues! I was praising and glorifying God in a language I did not know. Amazing! My family later joked that I didn't stop speaking in tongues for three days.

The Top Five Game Changers

The Holy Spirit has made a tremendous difference in my life. The Christian life is hard—the Holy Spirit makes it easier. Let me give you the top five game changers that the Holy Spirit has brought into my life:

1. **Power in prayer.** There is no place where our human weakness is exposed like the place of prayer. We don't know how to pray, we don't know what to pray for, we don't know if God hears us. We are weak. But the Bible says "the Spirit helps us in our weakness. For we do not know what to pray for as we ought, but the Spirit himself intercedes for us with groanings too deep for words" (Rom. 8:26). Once I discovered that praying in tongues is actually the Holy Spirit praying through me with perfect wisdom and perfect accuracy, my prayer life was completely revolutionized. The Holy Spirit knows exactly what to pray for, so now I always start my prayers with praying in tongues. Often I will sense a direction to my prayers as the Spirit leads me, and then I will pray in English. It's what Paul describes when he says, "I will pray with my spirit, but I will pray with my mind also; I will sing praise with my spirit, but I will sing with my mind also" (1 Cor. 14:15). The Spirit will help you in your weakness, guiding your prayers, empowering your prayers and

ensuring the accuracy of your prayers. It's the greatest thing in the world!

2. **Power in ministering to others.** Jesus said that the purpose of the Baptism in the Holy Spirit was to make us His witnesses (Acts 1:8). God wants to reach people through you, but you need power and anointing in order to be effective. You don't know the struggles and issues people are facing, but the Holy Spirit does. You don't always have love for your neighbor, but the Holy Spirit does. Once I discovered that the secret to reaching people was to let the Holy Spirit speak through me, life became an adventure. Every day I pray, "Holy Spirit guide me and speak through me," and He does! Just yesterday, I had an amazing conversation with a young man who had abandoned the faith of his parents and was seeking to know the truth. I would not have been in that spot at that time unless I had listened to the guidance of the Holy Spirit.

3. **Comfort for my soul.** I have a natural tendency towards anxiety and worry, so when I found out that one of the Holy Spirit's names is *Comforter*, I said, "Give me some of that!" Jesus promised, "I will ask the Father, and he will give you another Helper, to be with you forever" (John 14:16). The word translated "Helper" is *parakletos*, which means "comforter, counselor, advocate." The Holy Spirit knows exactly how to bring comfort, consolation and peace to our troubled souls. One word from the Holy Spirit can change everything! My habit before going to sleep at night is to recite Psalm 23 and to pray in tongues. Wherever I am and whatever I am going through, the comfort of the Holy Spirit wraps me in a big hug. I must say that I have slept soundly for the last thirty years!

4. **Guidance into all truth.** I don't know about you, but I'm not smart enough to guide myself into all truth. I need help, I need wisdom, I need guidance on a daily basis. When I

discovered that one of the Holy Spirit's main ministries is to guide believers into "all truth" (John 16:13), I was sold. "That's exactly what I need," I said. So I started asking Him to guide me. He usually guides me by leading me to a Biblical passage or Biblical principle. It's uncanny how precise the Holy Spirit is! Just the other day, I was seeking God in prayer, and the Holy Spirit led me to a Bible passage that I haven't read in a long time. It was like God was speaking directly to me. I ran upstairs and said to my wife, "How crazy is it that the Holy Spirit takes something that was written thousands of years ago, and makes it apply exactly, directly, specifically to our situation?"

5. **Victory over temptation.** You will face temptation, but I don't recommend that you face it without the Holy Spirit. Your flesh is strong and the devil is relentless, but God gave us the Holy Spirit to make us victorious in battle. The Bible says that the secret to overcoming temptation is to "walk by the Spirit" so that we won't "gratify the desires of the flesh" (Gal 5:16). Once I discovered this, I stopped obsessing about saying no to the flesh and put my effort into saying yes to the Spirit. As I worship in the Spirit and pray in the Spirit and am guided by the Spirit, the sins of the flesh lose their power over me. My heart is satisfied with the goodness of God, so I don't seek the paltry substitutes that the flesh offers.

Joe's Journey

My friend Joe was good at selling Christmas trees. Every year, our church sold Christmas trees as a fundraiser, and Joe would recruit me to sell trees with him. "You've got to pull the tree out and fluff it up so it looks full," he told me. One time, business was slow, so we were huddled inside the trailer to stay warm. "Do you believe in the Baptism in the Holy Spirit?" Joe asked me.

"Yes," I said enthusiastically.

"Ah," he said, "I can't seem to get it."

"What do you mean?" I asked. "You were prayed for and didn't receive the Baptism in the Holy Spirit?"

"Yeah," he replied. "I'm thinking it's just not for me."

"Well, that doesn't make sense to me," I said. "Why would God bless one and not another? When Peter gave the church's first altar call on the Day of Pentecost, he said, 'You will receive the gift of the Holy Spirit. For the promise is for you and for your children and for all who are far off, everyone whom the Lord our God calls to himself' (Acts 2:38-39). It seems clear to me that the Holy Spirit is for everyone."

"I don't know," Joe replied. "Maybe I'm too much of a sinner."

"Well that could be true," I joked. "No, I'm just kidding. That's crazy talk, Joe. No one is too much of a sinner for God. That's why Jesus died on the cross! I will say, however, that I've known people who were seeking the Baptism of the Holy Spirit and had to deal with something in their life before they received the Holy Spirit."

"Like what?" Joe asked.

"I was praying with one woman and she had to forgive someone who had hurt her and let go of all her hate and anger. It was not easy, but as soon as she did, she was gloriously filled with the Holy Spirit. Another time, I was praying with an older gentleman who said to me, 'I feel convicted of a sin that I committed years ago, Pastor Dave.' I asked him if there was anything he could do to make restitution. He said that there was, and as soon as he committed to righting that wrong, he was filled with the Holy Spirit and spoke in tongues." Joe nodded his head slowly and thought about what I was saying.

"What about," Joe asked, "those people who say that tongues and prophecy were only for the early days of the church, when the Apostles were still alive?"

"My response to that is simple," I said. "What does the Bible say? I simply can't find anywhere in the Bible that says God is going to stop pouring out His Holy Spirit."

"Doesn't it say, 'Tongues shall cease'?" Joe asked.

"Yes, it does," I said. "It says, 'When the perfect comes, the partial will pass away" and "for now we see in a mirror dimly, but then face to face' (1 Cor. 13:10-12), which obviously refers to heaven. So yes, tongues shall cease in heaven, because we won't need tongues or prophesies in heaven!"

"Understood," Joe replied. We heard a car pulling into the gravel parking lot, so we got up to leave the trailer. "Thanks, Pastor Dave—I guess I'll keep seeking." Joe's story doesn't end there. But before I tell you the end, let me say to you, if you are like Joe, and you have questions or doubts about the Baptism of the Holy Spirit, there are answers. Many millions of people have experienced the power of the Spirit, and the validity of our experience is beyond question. Keep seeking!

Joe Finally Got It

About one month after my conversation with Joe in the Christmas tree lot, my phone rang. On the line was a very excited Joe. "Pastor Dave!" he said. "I got it!"

"Got what?" I said.

"The Baptism in the Holy Spirit!" Joe said. "With speaking in tongues and all!"

"Really? Praise God!" I said. "How did it happen?"

"Well, my conversation with you that night really got me thinking. I went home and told God that I was sorry for doubting His goodness, and asked Him to give me another chance. I asked God to give me enough faith to receive the Baptism of the Holy Spirit, whatever it took. I began reading through the Book of Acts to build my faith. Last night, at the Sunday night service, we had a guest speaker, and guess what he spoke about? The Baptism in the Holy Spirit! I was like, 'This is my chance.' I went forward for prayer, and after about five minutes, bam! the Holy Spirit hit me and almost knocked me over. I was speaking in tongues all the way home!" To this day, whenever I see Joe, he smiles and says to me, "I still got it!"

. . .

THE HOLY SPIRIT is your secret weapon to living undefeated. The Spirit is God's gift to you. Don't leave this incredible gift on the table. Take it, unwrap it and use it to live the undefeated life!

Discussion Questions

1. What is your current experience with the Holy Spirit? Is He active in your life, or is He someone you rarely think about?
2. What are some doubts or questions you once had, or currently have, about the Baptism in the Holy Spirit?
3. Read Acts 19:1-6 and share your observations on this passage. How can you apply this passage to your own life?
4. When you read about the difference that the Holy Spirit made in Pastor Dave's life, which of the Top Five Game Changers do you find most compelling, and why?
5. What is one thing you can do this week to welcome more of the ministry of the Holy Spirit into your life?

12

FREEDOM IN FORGIVENESS

"Forgiveness does not change the past but it does enlarge the future."—Paul Lewis Boese

I HAVE NEVER SEEN anything hold people back from full victory like unforgiveness. And I have never seen anything set people instantly free like forgiving and letting go of past hurts and wrongs. Unforgiveness is a cancer and it needs to be confronted. A life of freedom and joy awaits you on the other side of forgiving your enemies.

"What are you doing, son?" my dad asked. His question surprised me, as I wasn't expecting to see him at the baseball field.

"Nothing," I said.

"Well, I see you're hitting balls into the outfield, but there's no one to retrieve them for you. Where is your sister?" My sister Kathy and I were best friends. One of our favorite activities was to ride our bikes down to the baseball field and hit balls to each other. But Kathy wasn't with me that day because I was mad at her. She had hurt my feelings by going out with some of her other friends and not inviting me. These were the days before Instagram, so I found out the old-fashioned way: I overheard her asking Mom for permission.

"Really?" I thought. "OK, we can play that game. I'm going to exclude her from everything I do until she begs to be my best friend again." I sullenly rode my bike down to the field alone, and pitifully hit balls into the empty outfield. I'd show her! My dad's appearance at the field made me realize how silly I looked.

"Did you two get in a fight?" Dad asked.

"No," I replied.

My dad wisely saw through my feeble response, and said, "You know, one of the greatest things I've learned in life is to let go of hurts. Don't ever hold grudges, Dave, it gets you nowhere. Let it go, and let the Lord handle it. God always has a way of working all things out for good. Do you know the Parable of the Unforgiving Servant?"

"No," I said.

"Jesus told the story," my dad said, "of a servant who owed the king ten thousand talents, which is like ten million dollars, a huge amount of money. The king demanded payment, but the servant fell on his knees and begged the king for mercy. The king's heart was moved, so he forgave the servant's debt. As the servant left the king's palace, he ran into a friend who owed him ten dollars. 'Pay me my money!' the servant demanded. 'Give me some time,' the friend begged. 'No deal!' the servant shouted, and had his friend thrown into prison until he could pay the ten dollars he owed him. When the king found out what happened, he was enraged. 'What? I forgave this man's huge debt and he won't even forgive his friend's debt of a few dollars? Throw him in prison until he pays off my ten thousand talents.' And then Jesus delivered the punchline: 'This is how my heavenly Father will treat each of you unless you forgive your brother or sister from your heart.'"[1]

"Whoa," I thought. "That's heavy stuff." I helped my dad load my bike into the back of our station wagon and climbed into the front seat. I stared silently out of the window on the way home, but I had already made a decision. I was going to forgive my sister. The minute I released my hurt and anger, a weight was lifted off of my chest. I felt happy for the first time all day.

"Thanks, Dad," I said as we pulled into the driveway. He thought I was thanking him for the ride, but I was thanking him for the freedom of forgiveness.

Forgiveness Releases Happiness

In the years since that night, I have repeatedly seen a direct link between forgiveness and happiness. Forgiving people are happy people. Resentful people are unhappy. Those who choose to live in a spirit of forgiveness towards others live in freedom and joy. You can't keep a forgiving person down, because even when life treats them unfairly, they practice the art of letting go and moving on. They are good at putting things in God's hands: "I release it, Lord. I refuse to hold on to bitterness and anger. You handle it, Lord!" Resentful people are always on the sidelines, looking at life pass them by. They can't understand how the forgiving people can be so happy. "How can they have joy, when this person stabbed them in the back, and that person told lies about them?" The forgiving people always have the same answer: "Let it go, leave it in God's hands, and move on." That's where true happiness lies!

The Four-Step Process

"But how do I forgive others?" you might ask. "It's so hard, and I try to forgive but never quite succeed." The fact is, forgiving others is a deliberate act that must be repeated many times. It's not a feeling. It's an act. God will bring the feelings later—you should focus on the deliberate act.

Many years ago, I was struggling to forgive somebody. I had been deeply wounded, and this person was totally oblivious to the pain they had caused me. In fact, even after confronting them about their actions, they denied all responsibility and said, "That's life." I had a choice to make. Either I could live with the weight of resentment, secretly wishing for something bad to happen to this person, or I could learn to forgive and move on. I came to the Lord and said, "Father, I need help. I know that I need to forgive this person, but every time I think about them, my chest tightens up and I want to pray down fire from heaven on their head. I know that's probably not your will, Lord, so please teach me how to forgive."

The next day, I was in my car and a Bible teacher came on the radio. It was a call-in, question-and-answer show and the caller asked, "How can I learn to forgive my ex?"

"Wow," I thought, "good timing! Let's see what this Bible teacher says." He taught the simplest, most powerful four-step process of forgiveness that I have ever heard. I applied it to my own life immediately, and it had a profound effect. I think the reason this four-step process is so powerful is because it comes straight from Jesus himself. He knew the human tendency to hold grudges and their terrible effect on the human heart. He also knew the incredible freedom that forgiveness brings to the human heart. Jesus wants you free, so here is His four-step prescription for forgiveness, from Luke 6:27-28:

1. **Love your enemies.**
2. **Do good to those who hate you.**
3. **Bless those who curse you.**
4. **Pray for those who mistreat you.**

STEP ONE IS to love your enemy. Not with your love, because you are not feeling much love right now. But God loves the person who hurt you. They are a soul for whom Jesus died. The secret is to ask God to give you His love for that person. You'd be amazed how this simple prayer will be answered. "God, give me your love for this person. Let me see them with your eyes."

Step two is to do good unto the person who hurt you. Go out of your way to show kindness to them. Send them a gift with no strings attached. Nothing will blow them away more, and nothing will free your heart more. I know you won't feel like doing good to them, but this is not about feelings. It's about obeying Jesus' prescription for forgiveness and living in freedom.

If you've gotten this far, don't miss steps three and four. These final two steps solve one of the biggest problems with forgiveness: the feelings of resentment can return. You forgive them on Monday, but you hate them again by Tuesday. Jesus tells us how to solve this problem! If you want to get free and stay free, simply practice the habit of praying for them daily. Every morning, call out their name in prayer and ask God to bless them, forgive them and lead them closer to Jesus. This daily practice ensures that bitterness never creeps back into your heart. Trust me, it works. This simple four-step process is worth more than all the books in the Self-Help section, if you follow it. Your soul will be freed from the weight of resentment and you will experience the happiness that has eluded you if you deliberately pray this prayer every morning:

"Dear God, I come to you in the name of Jesus. I know that I have sinned and don't deserve your mercy. But I receive it because of the cross and blood of Jesus Christ. I now extend that same mercy to those who have hurt me. Give me your love for [name]. I bless them in the name of Jesus. I ask you to forgive them of all their sins and lead them closer to you. I don't seek revenge or retribution; I simply ask you to bless their life. I release any hurt, anger or bitterness I feel towards them. I will not make them repay; I will bless them and release them. Now, bless my life as I go out into this day to represent you and do good works in your name. By the power of your Spirit and in the name of your Son I pray, amen."

Joseph's Story

Joseph knew something about forgiving wrongs. He certainly had reason to hold a grudge. His own brothers sold him into slavery when he was seventeen years old (how's that for a graduation gift?). But Joseph refused to get bitter and he worked hard, impressing all those around him. His master Potiphar saw something different in him. He saw that Joseph wasn't bitter and angry and complaining all the time, like the other slaves. He promoted Joseph to the position of overseer of his entire house (Gen. 39:4). Finally, God was rewarding Joseph for his faithfulness, right? Well, almost.

Potiphar had a wife who needed a cold shower. She got hot and bothered for Joseph and started chasing him around, begging him to go to bed with her. Many men would have jumped at the opportunity, but not Joseph. He had his eyes set on bigger goals and wasn't about to let an immoral woman derail his destiny in God. Unfortunately, Potiphar's wife took offense at Joseph's refusal to commit adultery with her and retaliated by falsely accusing him of rape. The next morning, Joseph woke up in prison.

Would this be the point at which you give up? If you are like me, you would be seriously considering throwing in the towel and saying, "What's the use? I try to do the right thing and God doesn't back me up. No more Mr. Nice Guy. From now on, I am going to hit others before they hit me!" But Joseph had a different spirit. He made a determination not to allow the rubbish of revenge or the hogwash of hatred to poison his heart. He woke up every morning and said, "I will not let bitterness or revenge rule me today. God has great plans for me and I choose to focus on the open doors He is placing before today. I will let go of the past and thank God for the good things He is bringing into my life." Long before Jesus revealed it to us, Joseph practiced Jesus' four-step prescription for freedom: Joseph loved his enemies, did good to those who hated him, blessed those who cursed him and prayed for those who mistreated him.

Forgiveness Benefits the Forgiver More than the Forgiven

I believe Joseph had discovered one of the greatest secrets to forgiveness: Forgiveness benefits you more than the person who hurt you. Very often, they don't even know that they have hurt you. And when they do know, they usually don't repent and seek restoration. So what? You need to keep your own heart clean regardless. Don't let them live in your head rent-free. Forgive them, bless them and move on with your life in the joy of the Lord. It's been said that resentment is like drinking poison and expecting the other person to die. It makes no sense. Stop waiting for that phone call that says, "Hey man, I realize what a jerk I've been. I was wrong, and I'm so sorry I hurt you. Is there any way I can make it up to you?" Assume that phone call is never going to happen, and you will be a much happier person. If it does happen, then thank God for miracles. But most of the time, it doesn't happen, and you are required to practice Jesus' four-step prescription for forgiveness. Accept this, embrace this and start practicing it today. Joseph did, and he was a happy man. He had every reason to get bitter. He had every reason to plot revenge. But he didn't like how bitterness tasted. He didn't want to walk around with the sludge of anger and hatred in his spirit—he wanted to be free.

Maybe in the early days of his prison term, Joseph waited for that knock on the door. He expected one of his brothers to show up, or Potiphar himself, and say, "We were wrong, Joseph. You can go free now." But he realized something before long: he couldn't live under the crushing weight of failed expectations. Day after day, when that knock did not come on the door, Joseph saw that bitterness and anger were only holding him back from serving God right where he was. So, he made the choice to let go of the junk. He made the choice to forgive and move on. Instead of ruminating on the past, Joseph began to wake up and say, "What do you have for me today, Lord? How can I bring glory to you in this prison?" He realized that life is a whole lot better when your heart is free from resentment. Even if his brothers and Potiphar never knocked on that door, Joseph was going to live in freedom.

Favor is the Result

The result of this choice was remarkable. Everybody wanted to be around Joseph. He had a contagious spirit. The Bible says, "The Lord was with Joseph and showed him steadfast love and gave him favor" (Gen. 39:21). Because Joseph chose to keep God first and not dwell in bitterness, the favor of the Lord was upon his life. Things went well for him. People trusted him. The keeper of the prison was so impressed with Joseph's character that he put Joseph in charge of all the other prisoners (Gen. 39:22). Instead of sulking in a pit of self-pity, Joseph was literally running the prison. He didn't have time to dwell on the past or think about those who wronged him, because he was busy rising through the ranks of management, and "whatever [Joseph] did, the Lord made it succeed" (Gen 39:23).

Think about what God could do in your life if you would let go of the past. Imagine the favor of God that would come on your life if you would stop holding on to resentments and bless those who curse you. Imagine the difference it would make at your workplace if people noticed that the Lord is with you. How would your relationships improve if people noticed that you love your enemies and you do good to those who hate you? I bet you'd would get promoted, just like Joseph got promoted. You would eventually get to the point in your life when others would say, "Whatever you do, the Lord makes it succeed."

Joyce Meyer's Story

I know that forgiving and letting go of the past is not always easy. There are times when the injustices of life keep piling up, and you say, "Lord, it's too much." Internationally-known Bible teacher Joyce Meyer knows something about the overwhelming injustices of life. She also knows the transformative power of forgiveness and the healing power of loving her enemies, doing good to those who hate her, blessing those who curse her and praying for those who mistreat her.

"I was sexually, mentally, emotionally and verbally abused by my father as far back as I can remember until I left home at the age of eighteen," Meyer told Charisma Magazine. At age nine, she told her mother what happened. But her mom did nothing. When Meyer was fourteen, her mom caught her dad in the act. But her mother was emotionally incapable of confronting the situation and left the room instead. "I was so profoundly ashamed because of this," Meyer said. "I was ashamed of me, and I was ashamed of my father and what he did. . . . At school I pretended I had a normal life, but I felt lonely all the time and different from everyone else. . . . What I learned about love was actually perversion."

After surrendering her life to Christ, Meyer realized that she needed to forgive her father. "I'm happy to say that God gave me the grace to completely, 100%, forgive my father," she said. "It took some time, but I was able to do it. God didn't get me out of the situation when I was a child, but He did give me the strength to get through it. It's true my father abused me and didn't love and protect me the way he should have, and at times it seemed no one would ever help me and it would never end. But God always had a plan for my life, and He has redeemed me. He has taken what Satan meant for harm and turned it into something good. He has taken away my shame and given me a double reward and recompense."

When her father was sick and dying in the hospital, God spoke to Meyer that she was to move him close to her house and take care of him. Meyer's husband Dave disagreed with the plan but allowed Joyce to make the decision. Every day, Meyer loved and served her dad, providing his needs and caring for him. One day he broke down in tears and called Joyce and Dave to his bedside. "I am sorry for what I did to you," he said. "I have wanted to say this to you for a long time, but I didn't have the guts. Dave, I am sorry I hurt your wife. Please forgive me." Meyer knelt beside him and led her father in the sinner's prayer. He then asked her to baptize him.

Meyer baptized her father on Dec. 2, 2001 in front of hundreds of people at the St. Louis Dream Center she founded. "I know that I know that I know, that God has redeemed, and what Satan has meant for bad, God has turned to good," she declared.[2]

Getting Past the Sticking Point

Many times in my life, I have practiced Jesus' four-step process of forgiveness. I determined a long time ago to live with a clean heart, and not allow resentment to build up in my spirit. But there are times when I am tested. Pastoring a local church involves pouring your life into people and having some of them leave you, disregard you and even betray you. It's just part of the calling. By God's grace, I usually handle it well. I bless the person, do good unto the person and move on. There are situations, however, that make me say, "Really?" I remember one such situation. I felt betrayed. It was by someone that I had trusted, that I had poured into over many years, that I had given a position of influence in my church. Those are the ones that hurt. My wife asked me, "How are you handling that situation?"

"I'm fine," I said. But I wasn't fine. I was hurting. I was allowing the enemy to remind me of my failures instead of reminding myself of what the Lord has done in my life and ministry.

"You will never build a successful church," the enemy whispered.

"You're probably right," I thought. Without realizing it, I was getting stuck. Because I wasn't dealing with the hurt and processing the pain, I kept tripping up on this sticking point. Things were going fairly well at the church, but we couldn't really move forward until I dealt with this one issue in my heart. When you have resentment or unforgiveness in your heart, your life will never fully prosper until you deal with it.

Around this time, I stumbled across a sermon video that deeply moved me and set me free. The young preacher passionately taught on Jesus' words from the cross: "Father, forgive them, for they know not what they do" (Luke 23:34). If Jesus could forgive the greatest injustice of all time, then how could I harbor bitterness in my heart? If Jesus' closest friends and confidantes denied Him in His moment of need, yet He still died for them, how could I let trivial things be sticking points in my ministry? If Jesus forgave the ones who had just driven the stakes through His hands and feet and never said, "I'm sorry," or "I was wrong," how much more should I forgive those who wrong me, whether they acknowledge it or not?

Here is the remarkable thing: as soon as I dealt with the hurt in my heart, there was a shift in my church. As soon as I fully released the pain and blessed those who cursed me, there was a noticeable boost in attendance and finances and the sovereign move of the Holy Spirit in our services. When you deal with the sticking point, things begin to flow again.

I encourage you to let go of your hurts right now. With God's help, love your enemies, do good unto them, bless them and pray for them in Jesus' name. Don't wait, do it now. How much freer would you be if you had no resentments? How much happier would you be if you had no grudges? How much better would your life be with no offenses against anybody? I encourage you to find out today.

Discussion Questions

1. Do you tend to hold on to offenses, or do you quickly forgive and forget? If you hold on to offenses, why do you think you do that?
2. Share about a time when you forgave an offense and experienced the freedom that comes with forgiveness.
3. Read Matthew 18:21-35 and share how you can apply this passage to your own life.
4. How would your life look differently if you forgave everybody all the time?
5. What is one thing you can do this week to promote a spirit of forgiving others and releasing all offense?

13

WE > ME

"God intended us to travel through life as a community. Think bus, not unicycle."—Bob Goff

IF YOU WANT to live in consistent victory, maintain close relationships with other people who are on the same journey as you are. The undefeated life is lived together, not alone. We are designed by God to need one another. In fact, He designed certain flaws into each one of us that are only remedied by close contact with other people.

"Trust me, you hurt people with your words," my friend Mark said. We were seated on a boardwalk bench on Belmar Beach. It was a warm night, and people walked the boardwalk behind us as we stared out at the waves and talked.

"You think?" I said defensively. "That's a bit of an overstatement."

"Listen man, I'm telling you as a friend," Mark said. "You come across as insensitive and people know you probably mean well, but they get hurt by your careless comments." Ouch. I definitely wasn't in the mood to receive Mark's assessment of me. Eight different defensive reactions were swirling in my head, including an attack on Mark's own shortcomings. But I held my tongue. I'd think about it and get back to him, I thought.

That night, when I got home, I had a talk with God. "Do I really do that, Lord?" I said. A verse of Scripture immediately popped into my head. The funny thing is, I didn't want that verse. I knew it by heart, but it wasn't the message I wanted to hear in that moment of my life. "Got any other verses, Lord?" Unfortunately, God stuck to His guns, so I shrugged my shoulders and opened my Bible to the verse that He had put on my heart.

"Let every person be quick to hear, slow to speak, slow to anger" (James 1:19).

"Slow to speak?" I thought. "But I like to jump in and nail my point before other people have a chance."

"Exactly," God said.

"Uff, I think we are done here for the night," I said. But, of course, I knew that I had to make a change. I worked on it and eventually God helped me overcome my critical tongue and establish the habit of speaking life. It wasn't until later that I realized the indispensable role that Mark played in this process. I never would have had the breakthrough in my life without Mark's challenge that night on the boardwalk. God sent a friend to reveal a blind spot in my life that was holding me back from growth. We are better together, and victory is only experienced in the context of intentional relationships.

Jesus' Small Group

Jesus had a small group, and so should you. You need two or three or four other people in your life who can love you and challenge you and pray for you. The first thing Jesus did when He started His ministry was to assemble a small group of twelve guys who would minister with Him. He called Peter, James, John and the rest, and said, in effect, "Guys, we are going to do this together." All of their learning, all of their trials and all of their victories would be together. Jesus could have spent His life alone, meditating in a mountain cave, and simply left us a book with all of His wisdom. But He didn't. He chose to transfer the totality of His wisdom and knowledge through the medium of a small group: twelve flawed yet loyal (with the exception of one) followers. They, in turn, spread Jesus' message to the entire world. If Jesus had a small group, so should you.

Peter's Breakthrough

I imagine some of Jesus' original followers struggled with the concept of a small group at first. "Can't we just learn this stuff in a class?" they might have protested. "Or can you send me a link to the podcast?" Peter was probably uncomfortable with the intimacy and transparency required in a small group. His first words to Jesus were, "Depart from me, for I am a sinful man, O Lord" (Luke 5:8). He wasn't accustomed to opening his life up to others. Before meeting Jesus, Peter's motto was, "Live fast, die young." He lived the rough life of a fisherman, and he didn't see the need for sharing his struggles or asking his brothers to pray for him.

"Your turn, Peter," Andrew said. The twelve were seated on a Galilean hillside as the sun set, discussing what they had learned from Jesus' miraculous feeding of the five thousand.

"All good. Great day of ministry," Peter said.

"But what did you learn?" Andrew prodded.

Peter looked down at his rough-hewn hands and paused. "Well," he finally confessed, "it showed me how much I need to grow in my faith. I honestly freaked out when I saw all those people waiting for lunch. I was like, 'Oh shoot, we need to order more chicken wings. This is crazy!' And then when Jesus told us to sit them down and tell them that lunch was being served, I thought, 'What lunch? We only have five loaves and two fish! I'm going to look like an idiot in front of my friends.' But when Jesus, like He always does, pulled off the miracle, I just started crying. I was literally handing out fish and bread through tears all day."

"Why were you crying?" Andrew asked.

"I think," Peter responded slowly, "I think it's because I can see how often I don't trust God. Jesus told us that He had it all under control, but I didn't trust Him. I just kept thinking about the measly five loaves and two fish. Then the miracle happened, and it hit me how often God has whispered to me that He has my life under control, and I didn't trust Him. I always try to handle things myself, and the truth is, it never works out. If I would just trust God and let Him handle things, I would probably see some growth and blessing in my life."

That small group was exactly what Peter needed. That's where he grew into the man he was called to be. Over time, his life was transformed from a knuckle-headed fisherman to a Spirit-filled Apostle. In the group, Peter was challenged and comforted and encouraged. He eventually became convinced that we only grow when we have intentional spiritual relationships in our lives. Peter became a fan of small groups, and a critic of lone-ranger Christians. As a top-level leader of the early church, Peter's advice was to "love one another earnestly from a pure heart" (1 Pet. 1:22). In other words, open your life up to two or three or four other people and do life together. Don't judge and divide one another—work together. Peter says we are like "living stones . . . being built up as a spiritual house" (1 Pet 2:5). His concept of Christianity was that every individual should fit next to someone else, and together build something beautiful. He had learned something from Jesus' small group: you can't do life alone. We need one another, and God is most glorified when we lay aside our differences and work together.

Better Together

Are you in a small group? Do you have intentional relationships in your life that help you grow as a Christian, or are you trying to do life alone? Humans have a long history of attempting to accomplish things alone, and we always fail. One of the greatest lessons that Jesus taught us is that we are better together. The entire focus of Jesus' prayer in John 17 is *unity*. He prayed, essentially, that we would see that the kingdom is only advanced in community. The story is told of the young boy who was standing over a rhinoceros that he had killed. A man saw this and asked incredulously, "Did you kill that huge beast?" The young boy proudly said, "Yes sir!" Curious, the man asked, "How did you, a young boy, kill this rhinoceros?" He answered, "How? Why, with my club." The man was still confused, so he asked, "Well, how big is your club?" The boy answered, "There are about a hundred of us in my club." In other words, the boy had learned the secret of working together with other people to accomplish his goals. If we would learn this secret in the church, we would be unstoppable.

Valerie's Story

Valerie was a member of my church who called me for advice. "Pastor Dave, I feel the need to grow in my faith. Can you recommend a book or a class for me?"

"I can recommend a fantastic book by Joyce Meyer called, *The Battlefield of the Mind*," I said. "But I have one requirement. You can't read it alone. I want you to join one of our small groups and read it together with a few friends."

"Oh heck no," Valerie replied, "that small group stuff is not for me."

"Why not?" I inquired.

"I tried that in another church, and I got burned by some backstabbing church members," she said. "It was so painful that I resolved to never open my life up again." So many people like Valerie fill our churches. They love God, but they don't love God's people. For them, Jesus is the best, but church people are the worst. Unfortunately, this is not acceptable. You can't love God and not love His people. The Bible says, "Whoever says he is in the light and hates his brother is still in darkness" (1 John 2:9). In other words, if you say you are a Christian ("in the light") and hate other Christians, then you are not really a Christian (you are "still in darkness"). Why? Because the essence of Christianity is love and forgiveness and grace. If we miss that, we miss the whole thing.

"I'm sorry to hear that," I said to Valerie. "But can I ask you a question? How's isolation working for you?"

"Well, to be honest with you, not so good. I know I need other people in my life, but I struggle. I don't know what to do."

"Why don't you give one of our groups a try? We work really hard to create a non-judgmental, gossip-free culture. We just want to glorify Jesus and grow in our faith," I said.

"I don't know, Pastor Dave," Valerie said. "I'll think about it."

Valerie finally did work up the courage to join one of our small groups, and she loved it. She made friends, she grew in her faith, and her life was enriched. She became such a fan of small groups that she started leading one herself. "You were right, Pastor Dave," she told me months later. "We really are better together."

The Benefits of Small Groups

Pursuing intentional relationships in weekly small groups has many benefits. Here are three:

ONE: You only grow in community. You can't grow alone. You can try, but you will hit a lid before long. The New Testament contains *fifty-nine* "one anothers," that is, commands that can only be carried out with and to one another. "Be at peace with one another" (Mark 9:50); "Love one another" (John 13:34); "Stop passing judgment on one another" (Rom. 14:13); "Serve one another in love" (Gal. 5:13). You can't fulfill any of these commandments unless you have other people in your life. That's where the growth is.

I know a man who thought that he could grow alone. He dropped out of small group, he quit his serving team and eventually stopped coming to church. He was convinced that all he needed was his Bible and a good head on his shoulders. Unfortunately, his good head got filled with weird ideas before long. Without the refining community of the church, all of this man's strange ideas went unchallenged. No one was around to confront his odd thinking, because he didn't allow anyone to come around. Instead of progressing, he was regressing.

Sadly, he is now completely isolated and has become a critical and unhappy man.

It is reported that Howard Hughes, who was worth $4 billion but spent his latter years in solitude, said, "I'd give it all for one good friend." The good news is, you don't have to spend four billion dollars to find a friend. Just join a small group.

TWO: Someone else needs what you can give. When you open your life to relationships, not only will you receive, but you will give. You will undoubtedly benefit from having others pray for you, challenge you and encourage you. You will receive life from them. But have you considered that you have something to give as well? Have you realized that someone else needs exactly what you offer? God has brought you through trials and experiences that have made you what you are today, and someone else is a few steps behind you. Wouldn't it be great to help them on their journey? Perhaps they can avoid one or two of the mistakes you've made. I'm sure they would be inspired to hear how God has brought you through the fire but you weren't burned.

Jackie Robinson was the first black player to play major league baseball. Breaking baseball's color barrier, he faced jeering crowds in every stadium. While playing one day in his home stadium in Brooklyn, he committed an error. The fans began to ridicule him. He stood at second base, humiliated, while the fans jeered. Then, shortstop Pee Wee Reese came over and stood next to him. He put his arm around Jackie Robinson and faced the crowd. The fans grew quiet. Robinson later said that arm around his shoulder saved his career. Sometimes that's all it takes! Be the arm on the shoulder that someone else needs.

THREE: The world needs to see our love. Jesus said, "By this all people will know that you are my disciples, if you have love for one another" (John 13:35). The world is so over dead religion. They don't need another sales pitch. In my experience, they only want to see two things: 1) a God who is alive, and 2) a people who actually believe it and live it. What if we actually loved one another in the church, instead of bickering and dividing? What if we took Jesus' command literally, and committed ourselves to serve one another in intentional relationships? I think the world would stand up and take notice.

Brenda told me how her neighbor Mary noticed that every Tuesday, cars of people would arrive at Brenda's house.

"Do you have some kind of group?" Mary asked.

"Yes, actually, we have a marriage small group," Brenda said. Mary asked if she could attend the group, and of course, the answer was yes. Before long, Mary started attending our church, and I asked her what she liked about Brenda's small group.

"I have never seen people care for each other like I see in Brenda's small group," she said. "One of the members had a baby, and they threw a baby shower for her. Another member had surgery, and they visited him in the rehab center. I must say, the love is real in this group."

What Holds You Back?

Do you currently have healthy relationships in your life that help you grow? You might see the need for other people in your life, but something is holding you back. Let me address a few concerns.

1. **I have been burned in the past.** I totally get it. People can be mean, and it hurts. But my question is, how long are you going to live in the past? How long are you going to allow what happened ten years ago impact today? Forgive those who hurt you, bless them in Jesus' name, and move on. Don't allow your destiny to be diminished by the hurtful behavior of small-minded people, especially when it happened years ago! God has great things for your future, if you can let go of the past. Why don't you try some new relationships? Everything you have learned in the past will only serve to make you better and stronger this time around.

God wants to take you higher, but only to the extent that you work together with other people. The measure to which you solve your people problems will be the measure that God will raise you higher.

2. **I'm not good at sharing.** Maybe you didn't grow up in an environment where people shared their thoughts and feelings. That's ok—you can learn. Many of us were told that children should be seen and not heard, and that real men don't cry. Now you know better, and you have the chance to make a change. While you can't go back and create a new childhood, you can start today and create a new future. You must open your life to other people in order to grow. You can't hold your cards tight against your chest and expect anyone else to trust you or open themselves up to you. Go ahead and take a small step. You might want to share your greatest prayer need with one other person, and see how good it feels to have that support. Once trust is built with this one person, God will open up more doors for you to give and receive encouragement and support in the body of Christ.

3. **My church doesn't have small groups.** I don't know how else to say this, but you might need to find a new church. Your mental and spiritual health depend on it. The days are over when church was only one day a week. Sunday is not enough! We need the strength and encouragement and refining that small group relationships bring into our lives. It's not easy to find a new church, but if your current church is not prioritizing healthy relationships, you might need to make the leap. I recommend that you visit www.arcchurches.com and find an ARC church in your area. I know from personal experience that ARC churches are healthy, Christ-centered ministries that focus on small groups.

How I Learned to Love Small Groups

I wasn't always a proponent of small groups. I remember when I preferred the anonymity of large group settings or the thrill of ministry teams, without all that sharing stuff. My experience at Bible college changed me forever. I was twenty-four years old when I moved from the Jersey Shore to Dallas, Texas. I didn't know anybody when I moved into the dorms, but God had plans for me. One of the first friends I made on campus was Jon. Jon and his brother Jeremy were from Houston, sons of traveling ministers. They knew all about talking the Christian talk, but admitted to me that they had to work on walking the walk. Through Jon and Jeremy, I met brothers Jorge and Phil, who also had an extensive church background but were still ironing out the creases of their own spiritual lives. The five of us ended up spending a lot of time together. God had formed my first small group!

The Bible says that, "Iron sharpens iron, and one man sharpens another" (Prov. 27:17). That's exactly what happened with this group of five guys. We had vigorous discussions on what the Bible says about sex and money and marriage and the end times. I remember one discussion we had about speaking in tongues.

"Do you believe that God can have you speak known human languages by speaking in tongues?" Jon asked me.

"Absolutely not," I said. "The Bible says they are 'tongues of angels,' so they are not human languages. Speaking in tongues is strictly a prayer language between you and God." I always thought I knew what I was talking about. Any Bible questions? Come to me. The only problem was, arrogance is not a spiritual gift from heaven. It was a character flaw that God wanted to work out of me. And He was about to use the medium of the small group to mold me and make be better.

"Actually, my mom was in church once before the service started," Phil said. "She thought she was alone, so she was praying in tongues. Afterward, a woman came up to her and said, 'I understood every word you were saying. You were telling me exactly what I needed to hear!'

But my mom doesn't speak the language that this woman speaks. God did a miracle and spoke to her through my mom's tongues."

Jon raised his eyebrows and looked at me, and then looked back at Phil. "Really?" Jon said. "What do you think of that, Murph?"

"Well," I searched for words, "what can I say? That's pretty dang amazing." As I walked back to my dorm room alone that afternoon, I had time to reflect. I knew God was confronting my overconfidence. I realized that I needed to stop talking for God, telling people what God can and cannot do. The Holy Spirit was way bigger than my tiny human understanding, and sometimes God decides to break the rules for His glory. "Forgive me for my cockiness, Lord," I said, "and thank you for bringing brothers into my life who help me to grow and expand my understanding of you."

EVER SINCE BIBLE COLLEGE, I have been a big believer in small groups. I have participated in small groups and taught others the benefits of small groups for the past couple of decades for one reason: they work! As long as you go into them with the right attitude, your life will benefit greatly from the intentional relationships you build in small groups. Your spiritual life needs to be sharpened like iron. Of course, don't expect perfection, because humans are involved. There will always be someone who doesn't talk enough and someone who talks too much. Overlook that. It's a small price to pay for the relational richness that will come into your life. Pray for God to connect you with one or two people in the room. Seek to build accountability relationships with them, so you can grow by the beautiful give-and-take that only exists in the Body of Christ.

∽

Discussion Questions

1. Describe your current view of small groups. Do you see the value in them?
2. Share one way in which small groups and/or intentional Christian relationships have changed your life. How have you grown?
3. Read James 5:16 and share how you can apply this verse to your own life.
4. How can you pursue accountability relationships within your small group and what benefit would they have?
5. What is one thing you can do this week to promote small groups within your church?

14

LIVING TO GIVE

"We make a living by what we get, but we make a life by what we give."—Winston Churchill

GIVING IS one of the greatest keys to living the undefeated life. If you want to live in continual victory, ask God to help you excel in the grace of giving. The flesh wants to grip tightly, the Spirit wants to give freely. The image of the undefeated life is the open hand, not the closed fist.

My Civic Was the Test

I didn't learn to be a giver when I was young. I saw generosity in certain people I knew who had money, but I thought, "That's easy for them. They have a ton of cash!" When I became a follower of Christ at age nineteen, God had to teach me about living generously. I started by giving faithfully in the offering at church (although it was not my full ten percent yet—that lesson would come later). When I moved away to Dallas, I had to sell my Honda Civic. God had been dealing with my heart about being a giver, but I didn't think the lesson was going to involve my Civic. My Civic was my baby! It was my first car, and it had never let me down. So many good memories were attached to that car, and now it was time to sell it. You're darn right I was going to get full market value for it.

Before putting an ad in the newspaper, I told my friends that I was selling my Civic, and one of them jumped at the opportunity to buy it. "I might just call him back and tell him that it's already sold," I thought, in order to avoid having to give him a discounted price. What a great friend I was!

And then God spoke to me. "Give the car to him," the Lord said.

"Whoa now, get behind me, Satan," I said. "I know that can't be God. The Bible says God shall prosper me in all me ways, and that doesn't sound like prosperity to me." But of course, I knew it really was God. I knew He was testing me to see if I would obey. I also knew, deep down, that God would bless me if I learned to be a giver.

I didn't tell anyone about it. I just prayed on it for a week to see if the feeling would go away. It didn't. So I gritted my teeth and picked up the phone and called my friend. He came to my house and readily agreed to purchase my Civic. When he pulled out the money to pay me for the car, I told him that God had instructed me to give it to him for free. He protested momentarily, and then started crying. With a hug, he told me that he had borrowed the cash to pay for the car, because he was down to zero. This car, he said, would enable him to work again and earn a living.

A Big Moment

As I stood on the sidewalk and watched him drive away, I felt as if God was smiling down on me. That was a big moment in my life. I must say that it felt great to be a giver—it was my first real taste of the joy of generosity. "That was fun! I could get hooked on this," I thought. But God wasn't finished with the lesson. There is one more part to it, as Jesus explains in Luke 6:38,

"Give, and it will be given to you. Good measure, pressed down, shaken together, running over, will be put into your lap. For with the measure you use it will be measured back to you."

Not long after giving away my Civic, someone came to me and gave me their car. For free. In the years since then, this has happened to me three more times. Can I get a 'hallelujah' in this house? You can't outgive God!

Consider this: everything you have is given to you by God. He is the ultimate source and provider of all you possess. He has the right, therefore, to ask you to give some of what you possess to someone else. He wants to use you to be a blessing to someone else. Don't hold on to your stuff as if it's all yours. Say, "Thank you, God for providing all of my needs. Let me live generously and bless others as you direct me."

Do You Have Money, or Does Money Have You?

Don't ever live for money. It comes and it goes. Don't ever set your goals based on money. Let your passion be people, not things. Money has a very dangerous power: it can grow tentacles and wrap itself around your heart. Jesus knew this, so He tackled this issue head-on.

> "And [Jesus] said to them, 'Take care, and be on your guard against all covetousness, for one's life does not consist in the abundance of his possessions.' And he told them a parable, saying, 'The land of a rich man produced plentifully, and he thought to himself, 'What shall I do, for I have nowhere to store my crops?' And he said, 'I will do this: I will tear down my barns and build larger ones, and there I will store all my grain and my goods. And I will say to my soul, "Soul, you have ample goods laid up for many years; relax, eat, drink, be merry."' But God said to him, 'Fool! This night your soul is required of you, and the things you have prepared, whose will they be?' So is the one who lays up treasure for himself and is not rich toward God'" (Luke 12:15-21).

This rich man thought he had money, but the truth is, money had him. He was under the spell of wealth and he didn't know it. This parable has one of the most tragic endings of any of Jesus' stories: "You fool—you're going to die tonight!" And his one problem? That he wasn't *rich toward God*. What does it mean to be rich toward God? It means that you put God first in your finances. You recognize that God has provided everything you have, and you are committed to honoring Him with your firstfruits, as commanded in Proverbs 3:9-10:

> Honor the Lord with your wealth
>   and with the firstfruits of all your produce;
>   then your barns will be filled with plenty,
>   and your vats will be bursting with wine.

Your Firstfruits

If you put God first, God will bless your life. It's that simple. One of the most tangible areas that you can check to see if God is first in your life is your finances. Are you giving God your firstfruits? Your firstfruits are the first 10% of your earnings. The tithe, or first ten percent of your income, belongs to God.

> "Every tithe of the land, whether of the seed of the land or of the fruit of the trees, is the Lord's; it is holy to the Lord. . . . And every tithe of herds and flocks, every tenth animal of all that pass under the herdsman's staff, shall be holy to the Lord. One shall not differentiate between good or bad, neither shall he make a substitute for it" (Lev. 27:30-33).

It's really simple to put God first in your finances: just give him your first 10%. That's God's clear and consistent command throughout the Bible. Just dedicate the first 10% of every paycheck to the house of the Lord. Easy, right? Well, not so much. Many people really struggle on this point. Because of the deep-rooted selfishness and unbelief within us, we don't want to obey God's command to give him the first 10% of our income. We would rather explain away this command, or ignore it, or modify it, or hope that God didn't really mean it. We like our money. And most of us don't have enough of it. So we come up with excuses.

The Excuses

Let me share with you three common excuses for not tithing that I have heard over the years (and even said myself!):

ONE: I can't afford it. This is what I used to say. And the truth is, until I made some changes in my finances, I couldn't afford it. I was spending 100% (or more) of my income, so how could I possibly give God 10%? Perhaps you find yourself in the same place.

I discovered the answer is the *law of firsts*. Whatever you do first is the most important thing. If you are a coffee drinker, you know that nothing else matters until you've had your first cup of coffee in the morning. With your finances, whoever gets your first dollar is most important. For me, the excuse of "I can't afford to give God 10%" finally fell away when I started to give God the *first* ten percent of my income, on the first day of every month. I set up an automatic debit to direct 10% of my income to my local church. That settled it. I never see that money. It belongs to God. And it feels so good to know that God is first in my finances!

Was it easy to live on 90% of my income? Heck no! I had to make serious changes in my family's finances. We had to change our spending habits, and change is hard. We had to aggressively eliminate debt. We had to set up and stick to a monthly budget. (For practical help in this area, check out Dave Ramsey's course, *Financial Peace University*.[1] I highly recommend it.)

Unless you make changes to the way you handle the 90%, you will not consistently give God the first 10%. Once I made the required changes in my financial life, tithing became a lifestyle. And I can honestly say, after many years of tithing, I have lived better on the 90% than I ever did on the 100%.

My 5% Plan

Now I need to be honest with you. It took me awhile to increase my giving to the full 10% level. When I was married in 1998, my income was rather sparse, so I got the bright idea of giving God 5% instead of 10%. I thought it was a great idea. My wife didn't agree. "But wait," she said. "I thought tithing was 10%."

"Well, right now all we can afford is 5%" was my wise and faith-filled response. I have since discovered that in God's kingdom, partial obedience is disobedience. But at the time, I forged ahead with my 5% plan. I wrote a check every week for 5% of our income and gave it in the church offering. I admit that I didn't feel right about it. I knew that the Bible (and my wife) said to give 10%, but I was in a duel with God. Have you ever been in a duel with God? I've had quite a few. And despite being stubborn, I haven't won one yet! After about a month of giving 5%, I stumbled upon a Scripture passage that made me lay down my weapons and give up the fight.

> "Will man rob God? Yet you are robbing me. But you say, 'How have we robbed you?' In your tithes and contributions. You are cursed with a curse, for you are robbing me, the whole nation of you. Bring the full tithe into the storehouse, that there may be food in my house. And thereby put me to the test, says the Lord of hosts, if I will not open the windows of heaven for you and pour down for you a blessing until there is no more need" (Mal. 3:8-10).

Ouch. I knew God was speaking directly to me. I was robbing God. That hurts to admit, but it's true. My excuses didn't matter. What mattered was this: if I was giving anything less than the full 10% to God, then I was robbing Him. Not only that, but my finances were under a curse because of my dumb 5% plan.

I only had one option: start giving God the full 10% and adjust my management of the other 90% so we could make ends meet. That's what I did. The very next Sunday, I wrote a check for the full 10% and gave it to God. It was a freeing moment in my life. As I placed the envelope into the offering that morning, I prayed, "Lord, you know I can't afford this right now. But I am going to trust your Word. You said to bring the full tithe into your storehouse, so that's what I'm going to do. I ask you bless my other 90% and let all men see that you never fail."

God has answered that prayer in so many ways over the last two decades. His blessing and favor have been consistent and unmistakable in our lives. Far from letting us go hungry, God has provided for us in surprising and unexpected ways. My testimony is that God has prospered us above and beyond what we could ask or think. You can't outgive God!

TWO: Preachers just want my money. Sadly, some preachers do want your money. But the overwhelming majority don't. The 1% that are in it for money are wolves and not true servants of God, and you need to stay away from them. The other 99% are good men and women called to serve God and pastor their communities. If they wanted money, they would have chosen some other profession. Pastoring is brutal. Not one of the hundreds of pastors I know is in it for the money. They are in it because they want to change the world for good.

This idea that "preachers just want my money" is a knee-jerk reaction to the fact that an offering is taken at every church service. "You see that? There he goes again -- asking for money! That's all this guy thinks about." The problem with this assessment is that the pastor is not raising money for himself. He is raising money for projects that will bless the community and reach more people for Jesus. It takes money to expand the kingdom of God in your local community, and the fact that your pastor takes an offering at every church service does not impugn his character. On the contrary, it shows that he is faithful to the call God has placed upon him to reach your community for Jesus. Your pastor is not pocketing the weekly offering. He has a board that sets his salary (and if this is not true in your church, I would not entrust my money to that church). I would encourage you to keep your eyes on

God and remember that the offering is really about your heart. Jesus said, "For where your treasure is, there your heart will be also" (Matt. 6:21). God is testing your heart every time there is an offering in your church. Where is your treasure? Do you own the money, or does it own you?

The truth is, the offering is your time to be blessed. Don't miss this. Jesus said, "It is more blessed to give than to receive" (Acts 20:35), so the offering is a time for you to be blessed by giving. Change your perspective from, "Oh, brother," to "I'm ready for a blessing."

A young couple at my church just started tithing, and they stopped me after service recently to share this with me: "Pastor Dave, we just need to share this story with you. My husband and I recently started obeying God and tithing the full ten percent of everything we make. It wasn't easy at first, but we were trusting that God would be faithful to us if we obeyed his Word. Well, my husband randomly ran into an old friend last week who is working for a large company that needs the exact services my husband offers. This company ended up contracting my husband for a job that increases our annual income by one third!" I have heard countless stories like this. You can't outgive God!

THREE: Tithing is Old Testament. Sometimes people try to pull out the theological guns and claim that tithing is only taught in the Old Testament and therefore doesn't apply to Christians. This is merely a deflection to justify the death grip they have on their money. It is true that tithing is taught in the Law of Moses, and Christians are no longer under the Law of Moses. We are not saved by keeping a list of commandments. We are saved by faith in the blood of Jesus Christ. Does this mean that tithing is no longer valid?

We could ask the same question about adultery or lying or stealing. Just because these laws were given to us by Moses, and we are no longer under the Law of Moses, does that mean there is no lasting truth in these laws? I think you would agree that adultery and lying and stealing are still wrong for Christians. So, how do we know which commandments of Moses still apply to us today?

One way to check the validity of an Old Testament commandment for the Christian is to see if it is mentioned in the New Testament. If it is, then we need to pay attention to it, because God is telling us it's an eternal principle and not a temporary law for the people of Israel. In the New Testament book of Matthew, Jesus tells the Pharisees that they should tithe. He says this in a rebuke: "Woe to you, scribes and Pharisees, hypocrites! For you tithe mint and dill and cumin, and have neglected the weightier matters of the law: justice and mercy and faithfulness. These you ought to have done, without neglecting the others" (23:23).

In other words, pay attention to the weightier matters of the law, such as, "justice and mercy and faithfulness," without ignoring the laws you are already obeying, such as tithing. In saying this, Jesus established tithing as an eternal principle that still applies to us today. He could have nullified tithing in this passage. He could have said, "That tithing stuff is so Old Testament. Forget about it!" But he didn't. He clearly and unmistakably said, "Keep doing it."

One final question I have for those who claim that tithing is only for the Old Testament, "Do you think that God wants us give less in the New Testament than they did in the Old Testament?" Now that we have Jesus Christ and the new birth and the power of the Holy Spirit and "every spiritual blessing in the heavenly places" (Eph. 1:3), do you think God wants us to give less than they did before Christ came? Now that we have the fulfillment of all the Old Testament promises and prophecies, should we be *less* generous? That makes no sense!

The Generous Widow

One time, Jesus and His disciples were in church. At one point in the service, Jesus saw something that grabbed His attention. He whispered to His disciples to pay attention and pointed to the offering box where people were placing their offerings. "Watch," He said. Several well-dressed religious leaders sauntered up to the offering box and, with a pause to make sure others were noticing their beneficence, dropped in large sums of money (Mark 12:41). They congratulated each other as they made their way back to their seats.

Then an old woman slowly approached the offering box. She was a widow who had suffered much in life. In her trials, however, she turned towards God instead of away from Him. She had developed a strong faith and a fearless obedience. She was willing to go where God sent her, speak what God gave her, and do what God told her to do. She was even willing to give away all the money she had to live on. "If God provides for the sparrows, He will provide for me!" she would say. Everyone knew her at church, because she never missed a service. And she never failed to give in the offering, because she trusted that God was a good father, and he would never let his daughter go hungry. As the disciples watched, this old widow dropped two small copper coins into the offering box.

Jesus turned to his disciples and said, "Truly, I say to you, this poor widow has put in more than all those who are contributing to the offering box. For they all contributed out of their abundance, but she out of her poverty has put in everything she had, all she had to live on" (Mark 12:43-44).

Jesus applauded the widow's faith and wanted everyone to notice her generosity. He told them to stop what they were doing and watch her act of radical faith. You might have thought that He was calling His disciples over to teach them a lesson on worship or loving your neighbor or prayer. Nope. He interrupted everyone's worship service to hammer home one unforgettable point: It's more blessed to give than receive, and the generous life is the best life.

I can guarantee you one thing: this widow never lacked for bread one day of her life. God richly took care of her every need. If she was willing to give generously, God would make sure that she never lacked. Just like the widow of Zarephath whose oil never ran dry (1 Kings 17), this woman enjoyed miraculous sustenance every day of her life. You can't outgive God!

. . .

Have you learned the secret of generosity in your life? Have you committed to giving God your firstfruits, and experienced the blessing that comes to those who give generously? It's fun to bless others. If you want more joy in your life, I challenge you to give more. If you do, I'm sure you will agree with me that the generous life is the best life.

∽

Discussion Questions

1. Do you naturally tend to be on the stingy side or on the generous side?
2. Share a story in which God used you to generously bless someone else, and how it made you feel.
3. Do you currently tithe (give 10% of your income) to your local church? If not, why not?
4. Read Proverbs 3:9-10 and share how you can apply this passage to your own life.
5. What is one thing you can do this week to increase the spirit of generosity in your heart and your home?

15

LIVING TO SERVE

"There is nothing more beautiful than someone who goes out of their way to make life beautiful for others."—Mandy Hale

"What the heck is Jesus doing?" Peter whispered to John. They were in the Upper Room and had just finished dinner. The disciples sat in stunned silence as Jesus rose from the table, put off his outer garments and wrapped a towel around his waist (John 13:4). When he began to fill a basin with water, Peter leaned closer to John and said, "There is no way He is going to do this." Foot washing was a common occurrence in first-century Israel, but it certainly wasn't something you would casually do for a friend. Only the servants did it. When you entered the house, dirty and dusty from walking on the road, the lowest-level servant would wash your feet in a basin of water and dry them with a towel. It was a great service to receive, but not to give. Who wants to get close to people's nasty feet?

One by one, Jesus knelt and washed the disciples' feet. What an incredible moment: the One worshipped by angels is stooping to serve. The One who should be lauded by all is washing feet. The One who hurled the stars into space is on His knees, scrubbing dirt from toes. "Why is He doing this?" the disciples thought. "What's His point?" Jesus didn't leave them wondering.

> "Do you understand what I have done to you?" Jesus said. "You call me Teacher and Lord, and you are right, for so I am. If I then, your Lord and Teacher, have washed your feet, you also ought to wash one another's feet. For I have given you an example, that you also should do just as I have done to you" (John 13:12-15).

The lesson was unmistakable and unforgettable. It was something the disciples would carry with them for the rest of their lives. And since that night, it has become a central part of the Christian faith: significance is found in serving. If you want to go higher in the kingdom of God, go lower. Serving others is the greatest thing you can do with your life. If you want to live in victory, take up the towel.

From Maserati to Ministering to Sick Children

My friend John didn't live for serving others in his younger years. He lived for himself. He had received an inheritance from a wealthy relative at a young age, and decided the best thing to do was spend it lavishly on himself. He purchased a Maserati and a condo in San Francisco when he was twenty-two and spent his days getting high and discussing philosophy with whoever would listen to him. "It was fun," he told me, "but I couldn't get away from the feeling of emptiness I'd feel at the end of the day." By God's providence, he stumbled into a church and Jesus changed his life. For the first time ever, he heard that significance was found in serving others. "That was new to me," he said. "I was raised to believe that he who dies with the most stuff wins." John joined the outreach team of his church and started spending his Saturdays bringing meals to the underprivileged. He discovered how fun it was to help those who had much less than he did. "Instead of going to bed empty," he said, "I felt happy when I could make someone else's life a little bit better." His real breakthrough came when he visited the Children's Hospital of San Francisco. "My world was rocked," he said. "I realized in that moment that God wanted me to dedicate my time and my treasure to help sick children." Over the past twenty years, John has donated hundreds of thousands of dollars to children's hospitals around the country, and now he builds Dream Centers (Christian centers that offer free care to the needy). John found his significance in serving.

Are You Really Too Busy?

Have you discovered the joy in serving? Do you dedicate time in your schedule to serving others? You might say to me, "Pastor Dave, I'm busy. I don't have time to serve." I get it. We are a ridiculously hurried and harried generation. But I don't want you to reach the end of your life and realize that you lived for yourself, and have nothing to show for it but a few bank accounts, an alienated family and some rusting possessions. Is that what life is about? I urge you to think higher and do better. God wants to use your life to bless others. You could start by signing up to serve at your church a couple of times per month. Or you could look into a community outreach and devote a couple of hours on a Saturday to making a difference. Push through the sluggish inertia of, "Nah, I could never do that." Yes, you could. The Bible says to make the "best use of the time, because the days are evil" (Eph. 5:16). If you live to 80, you are given a mere 960 months to live your life. What are you doing this month to make a difference in the world? I need to push you to punch a hole in your schedule and make time to serve others. Life passes quickly, and wasted time is never regained. I promise that you will never regret one minute you spend serving others and making the world a better place.

Greatness is Found in Serving

One time Jesus was told that James' and John's mother wanted to speak to Him. She asked Him if her two sons could sit on His right hand and on His left hand. She desired greatness for her sons, but she was going about it the wrong way. Jesus showed her the road to true greatness.

> "You know that the rulers of the Gentiles lord it over them, and their great ones exercise authority over them. It shall not be so among you. But whoever would be great among you must be your servant, and whoever would be first among you must be your slave, even as the Son of Man came not to be served but to serve, and to give his life as a ransom for many" (Matt. 20:25-28).

The road to greatness is found in serving. Robert Fulghum, who wrote *All I Really Need to Know I Learned in Kindergarten*, says he placed a picture of a woman next to his bathroom mirror. Every morning as he stood there shaving, he looked at the picture of that woman. The picture is of a small humped-over woman wearing sandals and a blue eastern robe and head dress. She is surrounded by important-looking people in tuxedos, evening gowns, and the regalia of royalty. It is the picture of Mother Teresa receiving the Nobel Peace Prize. Fulghum said he keeps that picture there to remind him that, more than the nobility of any nation, more than any pope, more than any chief executive officer of a major corporation, Mother Teresa has true greatness because she is a servant.[1]

Three Guidelines to Serving

You are the happiest and most fulfilled when you are serving others. Watch out for the obstacles, however. I have seen many people start serving and quit serving because they couldn't navigate around the obstacles. Let me give you three guidelines that will help you serve for the long-term.

. . .

ONE: Don't look for recognition. The key to healthy serving is to do it unto the Lord, not to people. If someone recognizes your hard work, awesome. If not, who cares? You are not doing it for them—you are doing it for God. Richard Foster, in *Celebration of Discipline*, distinguishes between self-righteous service and true service:

> "Self-righteous service requires external rewards. It needs to know that people see and appreciate the effort. It seeks human applause—with proper religious modesty of course. True service rests contented in hiddenness.... the divine nod of approval is completely sufficient."[2]

When you serve, don't expect anyone to notice you. Don't be like the man who looks around to make sure people see how much he is giving in the offering. Don't be like the woman who says, "Pastor, I don't need any recognition. Just a simple mention from the pulpit with my picture on the screen is sufficient." You are serving God, not people. I know it's difficult when you give and serve and nobody notices. It's so hard on the flesh not to be recognized! But maybe God is testing you. Maybe He wants to see if you will serve in the hidden place before He promotes you. Joseph spent years in prison, doing the right thing and faithfully serving, before God promoted him. David spent years in the caves, honoring God and serving his faithful team of soldiers, before God promoted him. Don't miss out on God's next level for your life because you refuse to serve in the hidden place.

For twelve years before launching Vital Church, Raquel and I served another man's ministry. It was a humbling, frustrating and hidden season of service. But we made up our minds to never speak one word against our leader. We were not serving him—we were serving God. If God placed us there, God would promote us when He was ready. Now, I'm not going to lie, there were days when I was ready to explode. "I'm done!" I would say to my wife. But after going to prayer, we would always conclude that we could not move unless God moved us. So we stayed, and we served, and we never spoke an unkind word. At the end of that twelve-year period, God began to open doors for us to plant a new church. It was amazing to see how people came to us, finances came to us and connections came to us. It was clearly God's timing. We launched Vital Church in March of 2013 with 160 people and never looked back. Thank you, God, for giving us the grace to pass the test of hidden service.

TWO: Don't quit if somebody rubs you the wrong way. When you begin to serve, you will invariably rub shoulders with other people in the serving process. Some of these people will rub you the wrong way. Don't freak out and quit serving! It's all part of your molding process. God is using the discomfort to shape you into the person He wants you to be. Don't run from it. Embrace it. Say, "OK God, this is kind of annoying, but I believe you are using it to make me better."

I once had a leader on one our teams at church who would do anything for me. He served and went the extra mile and loved every minute of it. But there was one thing he wouldn't do. I asked him to recruit more team members and diversify the labor, so his team would not be dependent on one man. Sunday after Sunday, however, I saw him doing the work alone. I thanked him for his tremendous effort, but insisted that he needed to expand his work force. When I saw that he wasn't going to recruit more people, I went ahead and appointed more people to join his team. I thought the problem was solved, but several weeks later, I noticed that he was working alone again. "What happened?" I asked one of the guys I had appointed to join his team.

"He is a great brother, Pastor Dave," he told me, "but he prefers to work alone. He won't let anyone near him." When I addressed this issue with the leader, he got angry and left my church. He was not willing to learn this one truth: we are better together! When God places you on a team to serve others and make a difference in the world, get ready to lay down your pride and work with other people. They may not serve how you like or look how you like or talk how you like. But stick it out—God is using the situation to mold you and make you better.

One time I received a phone call that there was drama brewing on another team at church. We had added several people to the leadership staff of this team, and apparently some fireworks were going off. By the end of the day, I had received four different texts from four different people with four different stories. So, I resorted to my favorite conflict-resolution technique: get everybody in one room and talk it out. Let's just say that there was some 'intense fellowship' in that room. But I'm proud to say that after talking through their differences, this team learned to humble themselves and work together for the greater good. They stuck it out and stuck together, and God used this team in a great way. Many people have come to Christ and are still following Him to this day because of this team's willingness to put aside their differences and work together.

THREE: Only serve within your giftedness. Life is too short to labor where you don't belong. The key to finding fulfillment in serving is to serve within your area of giftedness. "As each has received a gift, use it to serve one another, as good stewards of God's varied grace" (1 Pet. 4:10). That's God's design. He spreads out His gifts among all His children and expects them to work together to accomplish His kingdom goals. Have you identified the gift that God has given you? When you attempt to serve in an area where you have no aptitude, you make everybody miserable, including yourself. Your breakthrough will come when you identify the area in which God has gifted you. Then your serving will come from a place of passion and joy, not guilt and obligation.

When I was a new Christian, a friend told me that I needed to volunteer at church, because that's what good Christians do. Wanting to be a good Christian, I signed up for the only ministry that would take me: the youth group. I was told that there was a youth outing that Saturday. I showed up and informed the youth that I was helping supervise, so they had to do what I said. When they didn't listen, I yelled at them. When they tried to cross the street without telling me, I yelled at them. When it was time to go home, I yelled at them to get in the van. Inexplicably, I was informed by the youth leader that my services were no longer needed after that Saturday. The nerve! What was the problem? I had no gifting or anointing for youth ministry. I was a colossal failure because I was trying to function in an area where God had not gifted me.

If you don't know your area of giftedness, I recommend that you take an assessment. At my church, we use a simple tool called the DISC to assess people's personalities and spiritual gifts. Before joining a serve team, they take the assessment so we can steer them towards the team that they are gifted to serve in. It really works. When you are serving in the area that God has designed your giftings, you flourish, because your design reveals your destiny. It's my great joy to help people discover their design and run toward their destiny. "Wow, Pastor Dave, I never knew I would be so happy serving others in this area. God has made me good at it!" When you discover your God-given gifts and talents and serve in those areas, it's magical. You will bring passion and creativity and anointing to the job.

Fulfillment in Serving

Serving is not always easy, but it's always fulfilling. In fact, God has wired us to find fulfillment in serving others. Sadly, most of us spend years of our lives looking for fulfillment in the wrong places. We desperately try to squeeze joy out of things that are self-focused. We spend a ton of money on possessions and pursuits and projects that have nothing to do with making someone else's life better. We're missing it! The day we finally discover that life is about lifting others up is the day life really starts. A Chinese saying says, "If you want happiness for an hour, take a nap. If you want happiness for a day, go fishing. If you want happiness for a year, inherit a fortune. If you want happiness for a lifetime, help somebody." Researchers have discovered a link between helping others and feeling a sense of meaning in life. In other words, fulfillment is found in serving. A recent study asked over 400 participants to report on how frequently they engage in different altruistic behaviors (such as volunteering) and how meaningful their life feels. Participants who were more altruistic reported a greater sense of purpose and meaning in their lives.[3]

The story is told of the woman who went to a psychologist because she felt depressed. "I don't know what to do, Doctor," she said. "I have tried everything, and nothing works. I am still just as miserable and depressed as I was when I started. I'm frankly at my wit's end. Is there anything you can do to help me?"

"Indeed, there is," the doctor replied. "I have a course of action that works every time. Here is what you must do: leave my office, get in your car and drive to the other side of the tracks. Find somebody who is worse-off than you are and do everything you can to make their life better." The woman looked at the doctor like he was crazy, but decided to follow his advice. She found, much to her delight, that her mindset changed the minute she started serving other people. Her day was brightened, her load was lightened and her outlook was cheered every time she made a difference in someone else's life.

Stacy's True Fire

Stacy was a student that I had years ago when I taught in a Christian school. She was a sweet kid, but drama seemed to follow her. I spent an inordinate amount of time putting out the fires she started, and of course it was never her fault. It seemed like every day brought a new Stacy-fire, and I wondered, "When will this girl see that the universe doesn't revolve around her?" In May of Stacy's senior year, we went on a missions trip to the Dominican Republic, where we immersed ourselves in the lives of the needy for ten days, doing our best to lift them up and make a difference in their lives. As the leader of the trip, I was nervous about the possibility of Stacy-fires during our stay. "Lord, help us," I thought. On the first couple of days of the trip, everything proceeded without incident. And then something happened. It involved Stacy and it involved fire, but it was a different kind of fire than before. It was a fire of passion and excitement.

"Pastor Dave," Stacy said, "I am feeling something that I've never felt before. When I hold one of these poor village kids in my arms and give them medicine for their illness, I just can't stop crying. God is doing something in my heart. We are making a real difference here, and I think I want to do this with my life. I'm going to come back here and do this for a year after graduating." I had heard similar sentiments many times before. The emotions of the moment are powerful, but the feelings always faded when the students returned home.

But Stacy had discovered a fire that didn't fade. Once she got a taste of the joy of serving, she was sold. Stacy made good on her promise. Over many months, she studied the Spanish language until she was fluent, and the following year she got on a plane and moved to the Dominican Republic. She found that she was happiest when she was walking the dirt roads of a poor village, spending herself to help others. Stacy had discovered the secret that significance is found in serving.

USE your gifts to serve others. Your truest happiness and your best days will come when you make someone else's life better. Lifting others will become your passion and your joy. And then, when it's all over, you will hear these wonderful words, "Well done, good and faithful servant. You have been faithful over a little; I will set you over much. Enter into the joy of your master" (Matt. 25:23).

Discussion Questions

1. Describe the place that serving plays in your home. Is serving other people part of your family culture?

2. Share about a time when you served others and describe how it made you feel.
3. Which of the Three Guidelines to Serving to you find compelling, and why?
4. Read Matthew 25:31-46 and discuss the meaning of this passage, and how it applies to us today.
5. What is one practical way that you can serve someone else this week?

EPILOGUE

I was talking to my friend Dan the other day, and he asked me, "Do you really believe it's possible to live in victory all the time? I mean, we all have bad days."

"It's true that we have bad days," I said. "But even in our bad days, we can have victory. Paul and Silas were singing praises at midnight in the Philippian jail (Acts 16). David said, 'I will bless the Lord at all times' when he was running from Saul and living in caves (Psa. 34). In my own life, God has given me victory in the midst of my darkest days."

"What do you mean?" Dan asked.

"When my son was born two months premature, they kept him in the Neonatal Intensive Care Unit of the hospital. We weren't sure if he would live, and if he did live, would he be at a deficit for the rest of his life? As I drove to the hospital every day, I would pray and cry and worship. God spoke to me clearly in that season of my life, giving me comfort and hope and assurance. I can't explain it, but I had a buoyancy in my spirit. I had victory in the midst of the storm. And when my son miraculously recovered and never suffered any ill effects, my faith and confidence only multiplied."

In your darkest days, you can have victory. God has called you to live the undefeated life. Not just some time, but all the time. Your victory is to be continual, not occasional. I am praying that you take the fifteen victory principles in this book and make them a permanent part of your life. I pray that you live these principles and teach them to your friends and defeat the devil with them.

From this day forward, don't look back. God has new levels for you. Don't believe the voices of defeat that attempt to drag you backward. You don't live there anymore. Your calling is onward and upward. In Christ, you will not fail. In Christ, you fulfill your purpose. In Christ, you will live undefeated.

NOTES

Introduction

1. https://www.theguardian.com/uk-news/2017/nov/22/asleep-on-the-job-alleged-burglar-found-napping-and-covered-in-doritos

3. Upgrade Your Morning

1. Duhigg, Charles. *The Power Of Habit: Why We Do What We Do In Life And Business*. New York : Random House, 2012. Print.
2. http://ministry127.com/resources/illustration/personal-devotions
3. © Universal Music Publishing Group, Capitol Christian Music Group
4. https://hillsong.com/collected/blog/2011/10/music-worship/#.XCqHEy2ZORs
5. Müller, George (1984). *Autobiography of George Müller: the life of trust*. Grand Rapids, MI: Baker Book House.
6. (*Eat That Frog!* Tracy, Brian. (p. 2). Berrett-Koehler Publishers. Kindle Edition)

5. Discover Praise

1. https://hymnary.org/text/i_hear_the_savior_say_thy_strength_indee
2. https://www.azlyrics.com/lyrics/elevationworship/doitagain.html

6. God First

1. https://www.beliefnet.com/entertainment/celebrities/the-biggest-celebrity-is-jesus.aspx

7. It Never Gets Old

1. http://www.pursuegod.org/the-mechanics-of-bible-study-the-s-o-a-p-method/
2. Merriam-Webster.com, Merriam-Webster, www.merriam webster.com/dictionary/affluenza. Accessed 7 June 2018

8. The New You

1. https://www.joycemeyer.org/everydayanswers/ea-teachings/knowing-who-i-am-in-christ
2. Evans, Tony. *Tony Evans' Book of Illustrations: Stories, Quotes, and Anecdotes from More Than 30 Years of Preaching and Public Speaking.* Chicago: Moody Press, 2009.
3. "Who You Say I Am - Hillsong Worship Sheet Music". PraiseCharts. Retrieved 6 July 2018.
4. https://onelordonebody.com/2012/04/02/we-dont-need-a-power-encounter-we-need-a-truth-encounter/

9. Watch What You Eat

1. https://www.keepbelieving.com/sermon/think-on-these-things/

12. Freedom in Forgiveness

1. Matthew 18:35
2. https://blog.godreports.com/2017/06/joyce-meyer-overcame-abuse-by-her-father-led-him-to-christ-years-later/

14. Living to Give

1. https://www.daveramsey.com/fpu

15. Living to Serve

1. http://www.sermonsplus.co.uk/Illustrations.htm
2. Foster, Richard. *Celebration of discipline: The path to spiritual growth.* San Francisco: Harper & Row, 1988.
3. https://greatergood.berkeley.edu/article/item/can_helping_others_help_you_find_meaning_in_life

ABOUT THE AUTHOR

Dave is the lead pastor of Vital Church, a thriving community of faith in Toms River, New Jersey, that he started with his wife Raquel in 2012. Through his unique and practical style of preaching and writing, Dave encourages people to live up to their full potential in Christ and enjoy the abundant life that only Jesus provides. When he is not training for a marathon, Dave is hanging out with his four children.

Dave would love to hear from you!
Please connect with him at the links below.

davemurphyonline@gmail.com

facebook.com/davemurphyonline
twitter.com/thedavemurphy
instagram.com/davemurphyonline

COMING SOON

I am excited for my next book!

After writing Chapter 8 of *Undefeated* on the topic of our **new identity in Christ**, I realize that there is much more to say on this subject. So many people are living below their potential because they don't know who they are in Christ. When you see yourself as redeemed and forgiven and free, you live life victoriously. **Look for my new book in the Fall of 2019!**

Made in the USA
Middletown, DE
07 February 2019